Classical Engraved Gems from Turkey and Elsewhere

The Wright Collection

Sheila E. Hoey Middleton

Photographs by the late
Robert Wilkins

BAR International Series 957
2001

Published with updates to the text in 2021 by
BAR Publishing, Oxford

BAR International Series 957

Classical Engraved Gems from Turkey and Elsewhere

© Sheila E. Hoey Middleton and the Publisher 2001

Photographs by Robert Wilkins

COVER IMAGE see no. 8

The author's moral rights under the 1988 UK Copyright,
Designs and Patents Act are hereby expressly asserted.

All rights reserved. No part of this work may be copied, reproduced,
stored, sold, distributed, scanned, saved in any form of digital format
or transmitted in any form digitally, without the written permission of
the Publisher.

ISBN 9781841712482 paperback
ISBN 9781407353067 e-book

DOI https://doi.org/10.30861/9781841712482

A catalogue record for this book is available from the British Library

This book is available at www.barpublishing.com

BAR Publishing is the trading name of British Archaeological Reports
(Oxford) Ltd. British Archaeological Reports was first incorporated in 1974 to
publish the BAR Series, International and British. In 1992 Hadrian Books Ltd
became part of the BAR group. This volume was originally published by
Archaeopress in conjunction with British Archaeological Reports (Oxford)
Ltd / Hadrian Books Ltd, the Series principal publisher, in 2001. This present
volume is published by BAR Publishing, 2019.

BAR

PUBLISHING

BAR titles are available from:

BAR Publishing
122 Banbury Rd, Oxford, OX2 7BP, UK
EMAIL   info@barpublishing.com
PHONE   +44 (0)1865 310431
FAX   +44 (0)1865 316916
www.barpublishing.com

Contents

Acknowledgements	iii
Introduction	1
Notes on the Catalogue Entries	7

CATALOGUE

I SCARABS:	9
Phoenician **1** (ca.5th century BC)	9
Etruscan **2** (ca.4th century BC)	11
II HELLENISTIC:	12
Ringstones and cameo bead:	
Hellenistic **3** (ca.3rd century BC)	12
Hellenistic/Ptolemaic **4-5** (ca.2nd - 1st century BC)	14
III ROMAN REPUBLICAN and IMPERIAL:	17
Ringstones and cameos (ca.1st century BC - 4th century AD)	
Deities **6-16**	17
Bacchic themes **17-20**	35
Personifications **21-5**	40
Heroes **26-7**	46
Symbols, combinations & apotropaic devices **28-32**	51
Portraits **33-5**	58
Daily life & animals **36-9**	61
IV SASANIAN:	65
Ringstones **40-6** (ca.3rd-7th century AD)	65
V LATE ANTIQUE:	73
Cameo and ringstone **47-8** (ca.4th-7th century AD?)	73
VI RENAISSANCE AND MODERN:	75
Ringstones **49-59** (ca.17th-19th or 20th century)	75
Abbreviations	87
Index of Materials	93
Index of Provenances	94
Index of Subjects	95
Index of Inscriptions	97

Acknowledgements

I would first like to thank Sir Denis Wright for making it possible for me to catalogue his collection of classical engraved gems from Turkey, the former Yugoslavia and elsewhere.

I am especially grateful to Professor Sir John Boardman who has spared time to read the catalogue and comment on the text. Dr Martin Henig has also made some useful suggestions. Any omissions and errors, however, are my own. The photographs - a most important feature of the catalogue - were taken by Robert Wilkins and I am once again greatly indebted to him. 3M Dental (U.K.) kindly supplied 3M Express Vinyl Polysiloxane (7302H) for the gem impressions.

A number of other people have helped in various ways and among them I should mention: Professor David Bivar, Dr Dominique Collon, Dr Cathy King, Dr Simone Michel, Dr Dimitris Plantzos, Dr Gertrud Platz, Dr Jeffrey Spier, Dr Helen Whitehouse and Dr Erika Zwierlein-Diehl. I am also most grateful to Dr Andrew Shortland of the Research Laboratory for Archaeology and the History of Art and Dr Norman Charnley of Earth Sciences in Oxford who tested a number of the stones; as well as to Dr Sheridan Bowman, Dr Ian Freestone and Dr Louise Joyner of the Department of Scientific Research of the British Museum for their comments, help and co-operation.

Photographs have been kindly supplied by the Antikensammlung (SMPK) Berlin (**8x**) and the Kunsthistorisches Museum, Vienna (**25x**).

Introduction

SIR DENIS ARTHUR HEPWORTH WRIGHT, GCMG

Sir Denis Wright (1911-2005) was educated at Brentwood School and St Edmund Hall, Oxford (of which he was made an Honorary Fellow in 1972). In 1939 he married Iona Craig (1911-2006). During World War II he served in HM Consulates in Constantza, Romania (1939-41) and then in Turkey, at Trebizond (1941-43) and Mersin (1943-45). From 1946-48 he was First Secretary Commercial, in Belgrade, in the former Yugoslavia. As Chargé d'Affaires he re-established the Embassy in Tehran in 1953 after the resumption of diplomatic relations with Iran and remained there as Counsellor from 1954-55. In between two spells as Assistant Under Secretary in the Foreign Office he served as Ambassador to Ethiopia from 1959-62. In 1963 he returned to Iran as Ambassador where he stayed until his retirement in 1971. He was appointed an Honorary Fellow of St Antony's College, Oxford and a Council Member of the British Institute of Persian Studies 1973 (President 1978-87); Chairman of the Iran Society (1976-79) and President (1989-95). He was awarded the Sir Percy Sykes Memorial Medal, RSAA, in 1990. His publications include *Persia* (with James Morris and Roger Wood) 1969; *The English Amongst the Persians*, 1977; *The Persians Amongst the English*, 1985; *Britain and Iran 1790-1980, Collected Essays of Sir Denis Wright*, 2003; and contributions to the *Encyclopaedia Iranica*, the *Oxford Dictionary of National Biography*, as well as to the *Journal of the British Institute of Persian Studies*.[1] Lady Wright has described their life abroad in *Black Sea Bride*, 1997.[2]

Sir Denis describes in his own words how he started collecting intagli and other seals:

> 'I owe my interest in intagli to a white-bearded French bachelor, Gaston Malzac. He had been the French consul at Trebizond (Trabzon) on the outbreak of World War II but by the time I arrived there in March 1941 he had, owing to his support for General de Gaulle, resigned but preferred staying on in Trebizond to life in Vichy France. He was one of the very few Europeans there to hope for and believe in an Allied victory.
>
> One evening he showed me his little collection of Roman intagli and other seals collected during his service in the Middle East. This stirred my collector's instinct and during my 1941-42 travels along the Black Sea coast and inland I looked for *resimli taşlari* as the Turks called these 'picture stones'. In those days there were no antique dealers in what was then the back of beyond. I would, however, sometimes discover intagli in small saucers among beads and other tiny objects in the jeweller's shop to be found in every little town; shorn of their original gold settings they could be bought for the equivalent of a few pence or shillings. My most exciting find was in the remote village of Sadak, once the Roman garrison town of Satala (see T.B. Mitford, 'Biliotti's Excavations at Satala', *Anatolian Studies,* vol.24 (1974) pp.221-44) where a wizened old peasant woman produced from her bosom two exquisite red cornelian intagli representing Mercury (**11**) and Fortuna-Ceres (**22**). There, too, I bought a number of badly worn Roman coins and a brass Russian crucifix, a reminder of the Russian occupation of that corner of eastern Turkey in 1917.
>
> Later, when consul at Mersin on Turkey's southern coast, I found more Roman intagli, again in jewellers' saucers. In Yugoslavia (1946-48) I acquired a few more from small jewellers' shops in Split and Ochrid and from a Zagreb refugee living in Bari, Italy. Later still, when *en poste* in Tehran

---

[1] A full obituary appeared in *Iran* (Journal of the BIPS) vol.XLIII (2005) pp.v-xiv; others were in *The Times* (3/6/05), *The Daily Telegraph* (21/5/05) and *The Independent* (9/6/05); see also editions of *Who's Who* and *Who was Who*.

[2] I. Wright, *Black Sea Bride* (Square One Publications: 1997).

(1963-71) I added a few Achaemenian, Sassanian and Islamic seals to my very modest collection, mostly found in antique shops owned by members of Iran's ancient Jewish community.'[3]

The Collection

The Wright Collection is of particular interest and importance as the provenance of about forty of the engraved gems is known: more than thirty were acquired in Turkey and eight come from Republics of former Yugoslavia (present-day Croatia, Macedonia and Serbia). There are also several unusual gems among those without a provenance.

Gems from Turkey:

Asia Minor, or roughly the area covered by Turkey in Asia, has been a fruitful source of engraved gems and many are now scattered through various European and other collections.[4] A catalogue of the Yüksel Erimtan Collection has been published recently by Koray Konuk and Melih Arslan which is devoted entirely to a collection of about two hundred and fifty (mostly Roman) engraved gems, rings and sealings from Turkey.[5] Some years ago Marianne Kleibrink published an article on a large collection of sealings, including many official ones, probably from Doliche near the Turkish village of Duluk in Syria.[6] These publications give some idea of the range, importance and purpose of seals and sealings in ancient Asia Minor. Hellenistic rings of the 3rd century BC as well as later intagli from the west dating from the 1st century BC to the 3rd century AD (including a number from Aquileia) have also turned up in South Russia and round the northern coast of the Black Sea.[7] Although the majority of these gems were imports, it has been suggested that a 'number were produced in local Bosphoran workshops'.[8]

The majority of the gems from Turkey in the Wright collection come from the cities on the southern coast of the Black Sea in the provinces of Bithynia, Pontus and Cappadocia; others come from inland sites in Cappadocia (i.e. in central and eastern Turkey) or from towns in Cilicia on the Mediterranean coast of south-eastern Turkey (see map).[9] A few others come from neighbouring sites in Syria to the south. At the time when these gems were acquired in the 1940's, communications in Turkey were still

---

[3] About thirty seals (mostly Sasanian) acquired in Iran were presented by Sir Denis Wright to the Ashmolean Museum, Oxford in 1995 (Acc. no.1995.2ff); he also presented twenty Islamic seals and amulets to the British Museum, London in 1994, see V. Porter, *Arabic and Persian Seals and Amulets in the British Museum* (BM Research papers, no.160, 2011) p. 21, (Cat.633-634).

[4] See for example H.B. Walters, *Catalogue of the Engraved Gems and Cameos, Greek, Etruscan and Roman in the British Museum* (London: 1926) (abbrev. London); M. Henig, *The Lewis Collection of Gemstones in Corpus Christi College, Cambridge*, in BAR Int. Ser., 1 (Oxford: 1975) (abbrev. Lewis); and J. Spier, *Ancient Gems and Finger Rings* (Malibu: 1992) (abbrev. Getty).

[5] K. Konuk & M. Arslan, *Ancient Gems and Finger Rings from Asia Minor, the Yüksel Erimtan Collection* (Ankara: 2000) (abbrev. *Erimtan*). Recent articles in journals include: G. Platz-Horster, 'Kleine Praser and Chromium-bearing Chalcedonies', in *Pallas* 83 (2010) pp.179-202; Andrew L. Goldman, 'The Octagonal gemstones from Gordion: observations and interpretations', in *Anatolian Studies* 64 (2014) pp.163-197.

[6] M. Maaskant-Kleibrink, 'Cachets de Terre - de Doliché (?)' in *BABesch* 46 (1971). See also S. Amorai-Stark & M. Hershkovitz, *Ancient Gems, Finger Rings and Seal Boxes from Caesarea Maritima; the Hendler Collection* (Tel Aviv: 2016) for comparable examples to several intaglios in the Wright collection; Wright nos.3 & 48 were acquired in Kayseri (Caesarea).

[7] T. W. Kibaltchitch, *Gemmes de la Russie Méridionale* (Berlin: 1910) (abbrev. Kibaltchitch); O.J. Neverov. 'A Group of Hellenistic Bronze Rings in the Hermitage', *Vestnik Drevnei Istorii*, 127 (1974) pp.106-15; idem, 'Répresentations sur les Gemmes-Cachets. Bagues en Métal et Amulettes des Premiers Siècles de Notre Ère...' in M. M. Kobylina, *Divinités Orientales sur le Littoral Nord de la Mer Noire* (Leiden: 1976) pp.53-65; idem in K.S. Gorbunova (ed.) *Iz istorii Severnogo Prichernemor'ia v antichniu epokhu* (Leningrad: 1979) pp.104-15.

[8] S. Finogenova, 'The Collection of Ancient Gems in the State Pushkin Museum of Fine Arts' in *Index Thesauri Gemmarum Antiquarum...* (Moscow: 1993) (abbrev. *Pushkin*) pp.65-6.

[9] For the individual sites see R. Stillwell (ed.) *The Princeton Encyclopedia of Classical Sites* (Princeton: 1976); and maps of the Roman Empire in T. Cornell & J. Matthews, *Atlas of the Roman World* (Oxford: 1982).

Introduction

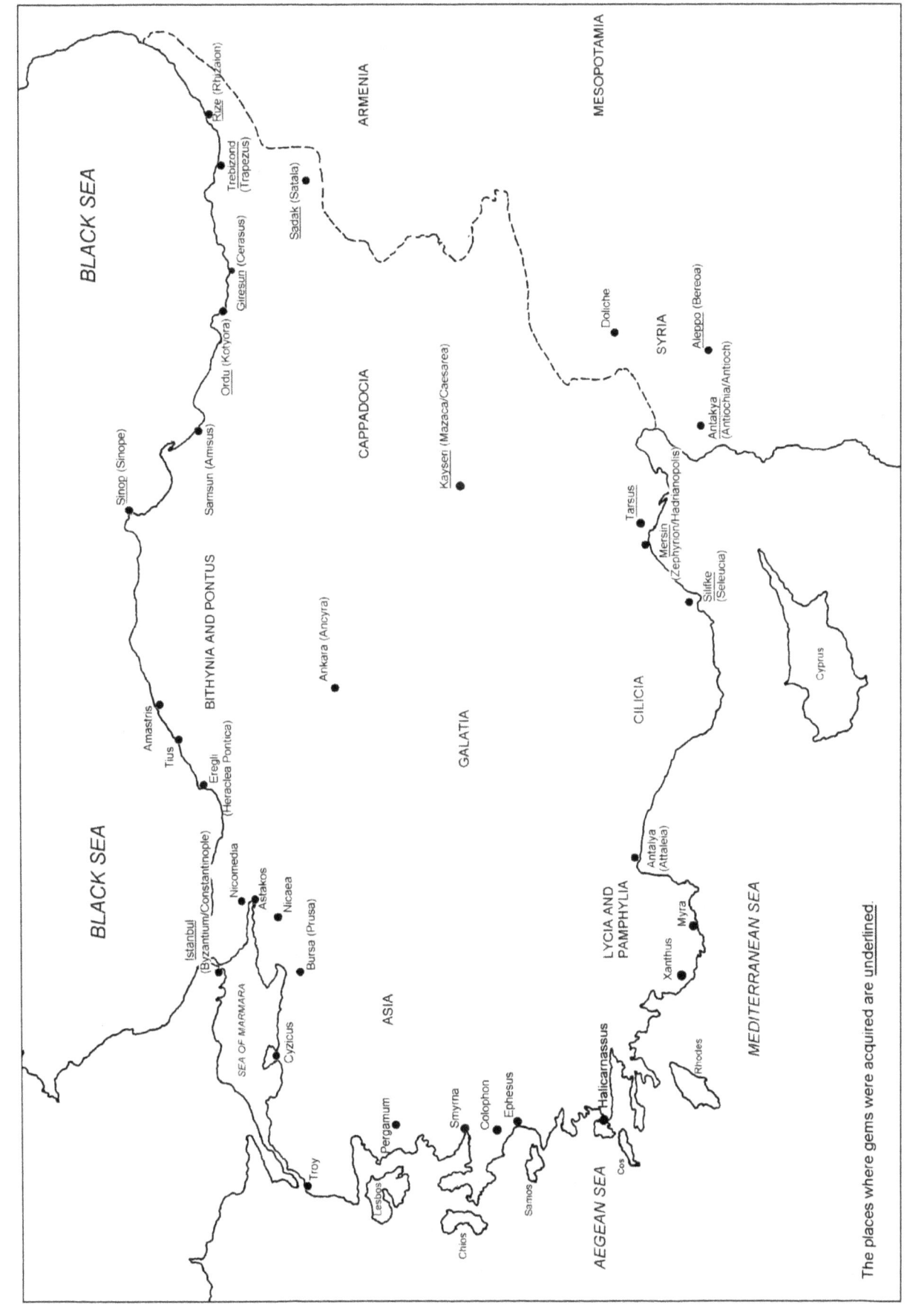

poor and many of the towns were remote and cut-off. It therefore seems unlikely that these gems would have travelled far from their original find-spots.

The earliest gem in the collection, an unusual 5th century BC Phoenician green jasper scarab (1) from the Black Sea area, probably reflects early trading contacts with Greece, which from archaeological evidence seem to have been active from the 7th century BC onwards. An interesting black convex ringstone with a worshipper or priest (3) appears to illustrate the mixing of Eastern and Western styles and traditions in about the 3rd century BC. Both the Ptolemaic garnet (4) with the head of a goddess or queen from Trebizond on the Black Sea coast, and the very unusual black glass cameo bead (5) from Mersin on the south coast of Turkey show contacts with Egypt and the Ptolemaic presence in Asia Minor in the Hellenistic period round about the 2nd century BC.

Soon after the mid 1st century BC Bithynia, Pontus, Cilicia and Syria were acquired by Rome; Cappadocia followed in the early 1st century AD. Most of the gems from Turkey in the Wright collection date to the period of the Roman domination and, like those in the Erimtan collection, the motifs most often correspond to types found all over the Roman empire - compare for example the two very similar intagli with pigs: the first acquired in Zagreb, Croatia (37) and the second from Giresun on the Black Sea coast (38); or the very popular and widespread motif of a dancing satyr (18). Although most of the gems were probably imports from Italy or other provinces of the Empire, a few do seem to reflect the history of the area and may have some local relevance - note especially: the Apollo with deities on a red jasper (8), Herakles and Geryon on a yellow jasper (26), and a cornelian, apparently without provenance, with a figure of uncertain identity which has sometimes in the past been thought to represent the Tyche of the ports of Amastris or Nicomedia on the Black Sea (25). Although this figure appears on coins (25x), this is the only example on a gem to my knowledge. It is uncertain whether any of the gems were engraved locally, but a cursory head such as the glass paste (34) might well be of local manufacture. The unusual intaglio of Theseus and the Minotaur (27) appears to be ancient but it would have been too large for a ringstone and so may have been an amulet or perhaps used to decorate some object. Several ringstones are especially fine or unusual, for example: the cornelian with a standing Hermes from Satala (11), the Eros holding a dove on a plasma from Istanbul (14), or the detailed and deeply engraved small cornelian with the Silenus head from Silifke (19).

There are two unusual Sasanian ringstones from Turkey (40 & 46). Henig has suggested that ringstones, rather than stamp seals, may have been more common in the Western part of the Sasanian Empire where Roman influence was strong.[10] Another two gems are of uncertain date but are probably late antique or Byzantine (47-8). Quite a number are rather later and belong to the Renaissance and modern periods. These perhaps date to the period of the Ottoman Empire or may have been brought in to Turkey by travellers from the west (49-59).

---

[10] M. Henig & M. Whiting, *Engraved Gems from Gadara in Jordan, the Sa'd Collection of Intaglios and Cameos* (OUCA: 1987) (abbrev. *Sa'd*) p.3.

Introduction

Gems from Republics of former Yugoslavia:

Eight Roman intagli in the collection come from the former Yugoslavia and these - apart from the Etruscan scarab (**2**) - fit in well with Roman examples already published from Dalmatia.[11] Several are fine or unusual examples of their type - note especially the following ringstones: a chalcedony with Zeus enthroned (**6**); a minute nicolo with Eros shooting his bow (**15**); a red jasper with Eros playing the flute (**16**); and a most unusual yellow jasper, finely engraved in patterned style, with two Fortunae or Concordiae from Split (**24**).

Gems without provenance:

Among the gems without provenance, several are especially interesting and unusual examples: a garnet (set in a modern ring) engraved with Hermes/Mercury (**10**); a plasma ringstone with Venus Victrix (**13**); and a small intaglio with a combination head set in a swivel ring was once in the Southesk collection (**30**). A group of Sasanian ringstones (described as 'Parthian') were bought at Sotheby's sale of Prof. A. B. Cook's collection of intagli on 15/1/1952 (**41-45**).

*

It is hoped that this catalogue will make a further small contribution to regional studies and, wherever possible, parallels have been given in the individual entries to other intagli with known provenances or to those from archaeological contexts.

---

[11] S. E. Hoey Middleton, *Engraved Gems from Dalmatia, from the Collections of Sir John Gardner Wilkinson and Sir Arthur Evans in Harrow School, at Oxford and elsewhere* (OUCA: 1991) (abbrev. *Dalmatian Gems*); idem. *Intaglios, Cameos, Rings and Related Objects from Burma and Java: the White Collection and a further small private collection*, BAR Int. Series 1405 (2005).

Wright Gems

Notes on the Catalogue Entries

Information on each object (scarab, ringstone or cameo) is given in the following order:

1. CATALOGUE NUMBER AND DESCRIPTION OF THE ENGRAVED MOTIF
The catalogue number (in bold) at the beginning of each entry is followed by the description of the engraved motif. For an intaglio the description is given as the motif appears in the impression, but for cameos and for some magic gems or amulets the motif is described as it appears on the stone itself.

2. MATERIAL AND DESCRIPTION OF THE OBJECT
After naming the material and the object ('*Garnet* ringstone...') a description of its colour and/or condition is sometimes given, as well as any other relevant details; and whether it is in a setting or mount. It is noted when stones were tested or analysed.

3. MEASUREMENTS AND SHAPE
(All measurements are given to the nearest 0.5mm)

Scarab: Length, breadth (of the engraved face and beetle), and depth of the beetle; diameter of perforation.

Cameo: Length, breadth and depth.

Ringstone: Length, breadth and depth. If the gem has a bevelled edge and the intaglio face is smaller than the overall size both sets of measurements are given (for shapes F.2,3,4,8). (Where a ringstone is mounted in a ring it is not possible to give its depth if the back of the bezel is filled in.)

Setting/Mount (ring): height (inc. ringstone) and width are measured externally and the ring or setting described.

Shape: For ringstones the code follows the one used by M. Henig (after J. Boardman and E. Zwierlein-Diehl) in *Britain* and *Sa'd* (see 'Ringstone Typology' p. 8)

4. PROVENANCE
'Acquired in ...' (the modern name of a town or city is given followed by the names of the ancient site in brackets), 'Ex coll.[ection]', 'bought' at Sotheby's etc.

5. DATE
Approximate dates are given where possible, mainly based on dated examples of similar style in other collections, or other evidence.

6. ILLUSTRATION
Scale: Scales are mostly 4:1 but are given with each illustration.

7. ENGRAVING TECHNIQUE AND STYLE
Where possible the engraving technique style and tools used are described. For Roman ringstones Dr M. Kleibrink's *Hague* catalogue has often been used as a guide.

8. GENERAL REMARKS ON THE OBJECT AND/OR MOTIF

9. PARALLELS FOR THE OBJECT AND MOTIF AND/OR STYLE
Parallels for the object and the motif and/or style on gems, coins or other objects are given where possible.

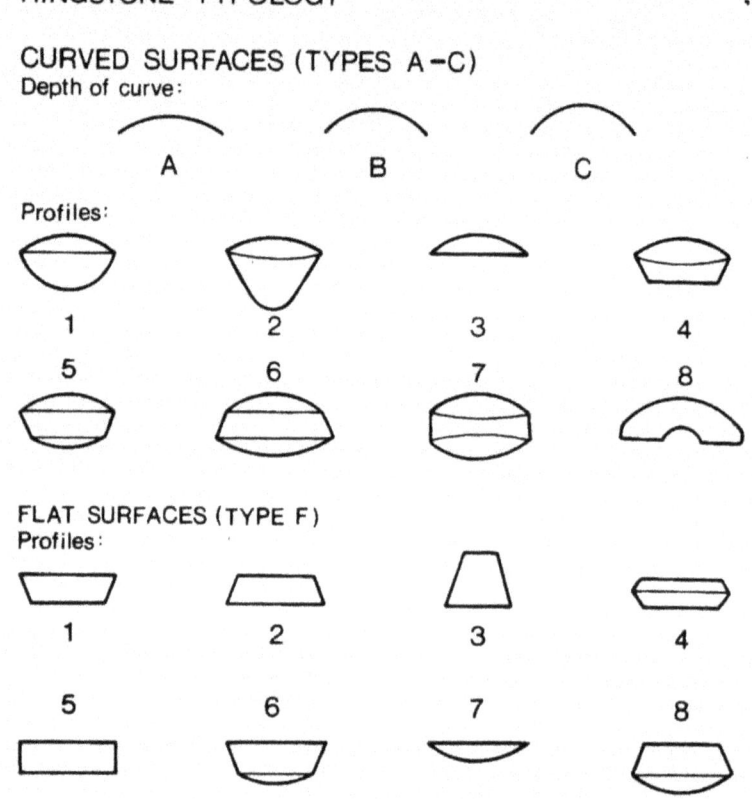

I SCARABS

1
A **scarab** with two signs on the base: a **Horus-hawk** or **falcon** facing to the left and behind it on the right a triple-stemmed **papyrus** plant with a straight central stem and a broken stem on either side; a plain linear border.

Dark green jasper scarab with diagonal white quartz band running through it (tested by SEM with EDXA system); a longitudinal perforation.
17 x 13 x 8mm; diam. of perforation ca.2.5mm
Acquired in the Black Sea area, Turkey
ca.5th century BC Phoenician

1   4 : 1

The Scarab: A V-shaped groove on the back of the scarab separates the head or clypeus (partly broken off) from the thorax and another V-shaped groove parallel to the first separates the thorax from the wing cases or elytra. The scarab has a plain gable back and thorax; the apex of the gable marks the division between the elytra. The legs are engraved as simple diagonal incisions which meet at a point half way along the side of the body. The beetle stands on a shallow, undecorated plinth.

   V-shaped grooves are found on early scarabs from Egypt and the Near East as well as on later Egyptian or Phoenician Egyptianising scarabs from Carthage (e.g. J. Vercoutter, *Les objets égyptiens et égyptisants du mobilier funéraire carthaginois* (Paris 1945), pl.4, no.120 - 5thc.BC, white hard paste, and especially no.133 - a 7th-6thc.BC glazed hard paste scarab which has two parallel V-shaped grooves). However, carination (in this case the gable back) is unusual on paste and green jasper scarabs of Phoenician or Punic origin.

The general appearance, shape and markings of this scarab seem to relate it to Late Archaic Greek examples which sometimes have plain gable backs (*AGGems*, pp.13-15). Compare:

Munich i, pls.65-8, especially nos.160, 164, 173, 175 - Archaic cornelian scarabs of the 7th and 6thc.BC; pl.68, no.308 - a Classical cornelian scarab of the early 4thc.BC; nos.164 & 308 have the usual ridge dividing the elytra but it is smoother and resembles more closely the gable on the green jasper scarab.

Berlin, pl.20, nos.101-2, 104 - a banded agate and cornelian scarabs, all late 6thc.BC Greek scarabs with incised legs; pl. 32, no.136 - a 6thc.BC Greco-Phoenician green jasper scarab with incised legs.

The motif: The hawk (often with a flail) which is the symbol of the god Horus and the triple-stemmed papyrus plant (sometimes identified as a lotus plant) are purely Egyptian motifs and are common on Egyptian and Phoenician scarabs (see A.H.Gardiner, *Egyptian Grammar* (1957), Sign List, p.467, G.5; and p.481, M.15 & 16). On a faience scarab of the 25th Dynasty with the same two signs, Rowe suggests that the meaning may be 'King of Lower Egypt' - because the papyrus clump is the emblem of Lower Egypt and the ruler can be represented as Horus (A. Rowe, *A Catalogue of Egyptian Scarabs in the Palestine Archaeological Museum* (1936) p.207, no.883). Vercoutter interprets them rather differently (Vercoutter, op.cit., pp.81, 85). In any case, it seems most likely that the signs on this scarab would have been regarded as a simple protective magic formula.

The hawk and papyrus plant appear together in a horizontal arrangement on a number of faience scarabs found at Carthage where this motif seems to have been particularly popular:

Vercoutter, op.cit. nos.90-91 - coloured paste scarabs; on the base, a hawk facing a triple-stemmed plant; nos.89, 92 - similar but with additional symbols (see Gorton op.cit below).

L. Delaporte, *Musée du Louvre, Catalogue des Cylindres orientaux* i, *Fouilles et Missions* (Paris: 1920) pl.59, fig.32 - the two signs with an egg above.

A.F Gorton, *Egyptian and Egyptianizing Scarabs, A Typology of steatite, faience and paste scarabs from Punic and other Mediterranean sites* (Oxford: 1996) pp.112-3, no.3; pp.129-30, no.29 (= Vercoutter, op.cit., nos.92 & 89).

Many of the paste scarabs found at Carthage were imports from Naukratis in the Nile Delta where they were mass-produced for export about the beginning of the 6th century BC (see J. Boardman, *The Greeks Overseas; their Colonies and Trade*, 4th ed. (1999) p.118ff. & esp. p.126ff. for the scarab factory). Naukratis was a centre for Greek traders and scarabs from there have also been found in Greece and Greek settlements abroad - including sites round the Black Sea (see Gorton, pp.91-2, 174, 177-80, 184). These two symbols (sometimes with other signs) also appeared on slightly earlier scarabs from Carthage which probably predate the Naukratis factory and which may have come from elsewhere in Egypt (see Gorton, op.cit., pp.82-3, nos.24, 37, p.84, no.17 (= Vercoutter, op.cit., nos.412, 411, 395); pp.86-7, no.7 (= Vercoutter, op.cit. no.247) - 7th-6thc.BC).

The Horus-hawk sometimes standing on a three-stemmed papyrus but arranged vertically and often accompanied by other symbols is found on green jasper scarabs of Sardinian type. However, these are all very different both in iconography and engraving style to this example from the Black Sea area. The distinctive 'segmented' treatment of the Horus-hawk also seems unusual on Phoenician scarabs but an owl on a paste scarab with Egyptian hieroglyphs dated to ca.6th century BC from Ibiza is also segmented - though rather differently (J.H. Fernandez & J. Padro, *Escarabeos del Museo Arqueologico de Ibiza* (Madrid 1982) pp.25-8, no.2, and cover ill.; and nos.21-2 for the vertical arrangement with the hawk standing on a papyrus or 'lotus').

The earliest scarabs found on Greek sites round the Black Sea date from the late 7th and early 6th century BC, the period of the expansion of Greek trade in the area. No close parallel for this scarab has come to my notice; the shallow engraving, segmented treatment of the hawk and stylisation of the plant are all unusual. However, the motifs do suggest that it may have been copied from a faience scarab of the type exported to Greece or Greek settlements from the Naukratis factory after 620 BC. Both the style of the beetle and the motif appear to be late. This scarab therefore, like the stone scarabs from Carthage, should probably be dated slightly later than the paste examples - i.e. to ca.5th-4th century BC.

2

A **scarab** with a crouching **lion** on the base enclosed in a cross-hatched border; the lion's head is turned back to the right and its mouth is open with its tongue hanging out; a long tail curves over its back; it has a mane and its ribs are marked.

Cornelian scarab, dark reddish-brown; the remains of a bronze swivel in the perforation.
12 x 7.5 x 5mm; diam. of perforation ca.1.5mm
Bought in Bari, 1946 (?acquired in Zagreb, Croatia; see p.1)
ca.3rd century BC Etruscan

4 : 1

2

The scarab: the head is dentate with a hatched semi-circle behind and a plain deep groove dividing it from the thorax; two curved parallel lines with hatching between them divide the thorax from the elytra; the division between the elytra is marked by two parallel incised lines and the winglets are shown as three oblique parallel lines on either side. The six legs of the scarab have been left in relief (unlike those on **1** which are incised); the front legs have diagonal grooves and the two behind have single grooves running along their length (cf. *Oxford*, no.228, p.56). The narrow plinth has fine vertical hatching. This beetle is very close to an example dated to the first half of the 3rd century BC in *Berlin*, pl.50, no.290. For a description of the different characteristics of Archaic Greek, Phoenician and Etruscan scarab beetles, see *AGGems*, pp.13-17.

The motif: although the quadruped on the base somewhat resembles a dog with its pointed snout and ears (cf. *Vienna* i, no.88; *Getty*, nos.158-9), a lion is probably intended. Its mane is indicated by several grooves, there seem to be claws on its paws and lions sometimes have their tongues hanging out (e.g. *AGGems*, no.403). The snout, joints and paws are marked by round drill holes, typical of the *a globolo* style of later Etruscan scarabs (*Oxford*, pp.48-9). The body of the lion is highly polished and the scarab is in perfect condition.

Compare the following Etruscan scarabs:
Vienna i, no.53 - 4thc.BC, a more naturalistic representation of a lion.
Thorvaldsen, no.45 - a similar lion with a pointed snout preparing to spring; engraved in an earlier style.
Intaglios and Rings, no.194 - a lion in similar style.

II HELLENISTIC INTAGLI

3
A **bearded priest** or **worshipper** in long robe and wearing a scull-cap stands in profile facing left in front of a plant (perhaps corn); he raises his right hand in a gesture of adoration and a holds a long sceptre in his left hand. Ground line.

Black serpentinite (magnesium silicate) ringstone (with areas of calcite and quartz; and traces of nickel and iron; tested by SEM with EDXA system); smooth, polished face, but the surface is rougher round the edge.
22 x 13.5 x 6.5mm. Shape A.4 (but with ca.2mm almost vertical sides, as *Vienna* i, p.15, 6b)
Acquired in Kayseri (Mazaca/Caesarea), Cappadocia, central Turkey (October 1943)
ca. 4th-3rd century BC Hellenistic or later?

3   4 : 1

The stone shows some signs of wear and it is rather rough round the edge - perhaps where it was held in the setting. However, the figure and the surrounding area is highly polished. This is an unusual intaglio; both the shape of the ringstone and engraving style is Hellenistic but the worshipping figure is Babylonian in type. There are small converging diagonal grooves at the top of the stalk which suggests that the plant probably represents corn.

Standing figures with their right hand raised in a gesture of blessing or adoration holding either a sceptre or with a plant belong to the oriental iconographic repertoire and date back to the early first millennium BC. The type continues into the Persian and Hellenistic periods (*Karthago* 3: *Die Deutschen Ausgrabungen in Karthago* ed. F. Racob *et al.* (1999) no.164, pp.36, 81 (below).

Rings for sealing had already been introduced into Mesopotamia from the West in the Achaemenid period (5th century BC) and continued after the conquest of Alexander the Great. Both Greek and Eastern themes were used and some sealings of Eastern type show Greek influence (see L. Legrain, *The Culture of the Babylonians from their Seals in the Collections of the Museum* (Publications of the Babylonian Section 14; Philadelphia, 1925) pp.45-9; L. Bregstein, 'Sealing Practices in the Fifth Century BC. Miraŝu Archive from Nippur, Iraq', *BCH Suppl.* 29

II Hellenistic

(1996) pp.55-6, pl.10). This intaglio illustrates another aspect of the mixing of styles and traditions and perhaps shows a Westerner's attempt to copy the motif from a Babylonian relief, seal or perhaps sealing (worshipping figures usually face to the right in impression rather than on the stone itself - cf. figures of similar type, Legrain op.cit., pl.45, no.956ff.).

Compare the worshippers:
Karthago 3, op.cit., no.164 - 4thc. BC flat clay sealing; the impression is made with a ring bezel; a figure of similar appearance to the one on the intaglio from Kayseri faces to the right in impression with right hand raised and left hand holding an upright sceptre with ovoid end.
  no.165 - 4th-3rdc.BC sealing; a similar figure but without the sceptre.
Legrain, op.cit. 1925, no.970 (=L. Bregstein, op.cit. - pl.10) - a female figure or worshipper brings a branch (or barley) as an offering; impression made by a western style ring; 5thc.BC.
L. Jakob-Rost, *Die Stempelsiegel im Vorderasiatischen Museum* (Berlin: 1975), pl.10, no.199 - an alabaster scaraboid with worshipping figures; on one side of the seal is a female figure with a plant behind (Assyrian-Babylonian).

4

Bust of **Aphrodite/Venus** or **Arsinoe III** (?) in profile to the right; her hair, shown as fine parallel S-shaped wavy lines, is arranged in a soft roll to frame her face and is gathered into a low bun on her neck; she wears a *stephane*, earrings and a necklace of spherical beads; a few folds of her mantle are visible at her neck.

Garnet ringstone; diagonal fracture (mended) and a large triangular chip out of the right edge.
18 x 14 x 4.5mm. Shape F.7 irregular (in profile the stone tapers towards the lower end)
Acquired in Trabzon/Trebizond (Trapezus) on the southern coast of the Black Sea, Turkey (1942)
Early 2nd century BC Hellenistic/Ptolemaic

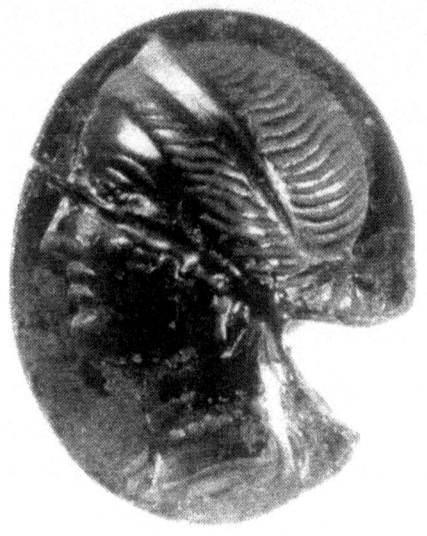

4   4 : 1

The features of the queen or goddess are subtly drawn: the outline of her nose is a fine straight line with a deeper groove for the nostril, and her mouth is marked as two round drill holes with very short diagonal grooves in the corner; the different planes of her forehead, cheek and chin are smoothly modelled and contrast with the fine linear engraving of her wavy hair; soft folds are just visible on her neck indicating the 'rings of Venus'.

A group of about fifty late engraved garnets of this shape (flat face and convex back) depicting Tyches, deities or possibly Ptolemaic kings and queens have been identified and dated to the 1st and 2nd centuries BC - see J. Spier, 'A Group of Ptolemaic Engraved Garnets' in *Journal of the Walters Art Gallery* 47 (1989) p.21ff; and Plantzos, *Hellenistic*, pp.78-80 who believes that the majority of these garnets come from the Levantine coast. The quality of engraving of this gem from Trebizond, however, is rather better than most examples in the group.

A very fine convex garnet from Kos set in an ancient gold ring is almost certainly a portrait of the Ptolemaic queen Arsinoe III Philopator, ca.235-203 BC, and is dated to the last quarter of the 3rd century BC (see Plantzos, *Hellenistic*, pl.6.33, p.49 (= *Vienna* i, no.32); cf. also pl.7.35 (= Spier op.cit. no.1) - a fine portrait in Boston). Rulers were thought of as living gods and so they were often assimilated to deities or actually identified with them. The Vienna gem corresponds closely to coin types of Arsinoe III who was portrayed as Aphrodite (identified by her *stephane* and jewellery) on her own coinage (Plantzos, *Hellenistic*, pl.93.14, pp.49-50). Among the gems related to the Vienna portrait on the convex stone is another garnet with a flat face and convex back (Plantzos, *Hellenistic*, pl.7.36, p.50). This is very similar to the Trebizond example except that it is unclear whether the goddess wears a necklace made up of small pendants or has a decorated collar. The engraving on the Trebizond gem is less rigid and linear and the goddess's features seem softer which relates her more closely to the Vienna Royal portrait. It is, however, uncertain

II Hellenistic

whether a goddess or a queen is represented on the two flat garnets; perhaps they simply illustrate a general type used for Ptolemaic queens who wished to be represented as Aphrodite rather than an actual portrait of Arsinoe III.

Ptolemaic engraved garnets have been found in Syria, Phoenicia and Egypt as well as other areas under Ptolemaic control. It has been suggested they were used as official seals by Ptolemaic envoys sent abroad (cf. *Oxford*, pp.82-3), used as gifts or traded. Some fine portraits on garnets of this shape (flat face, convex back) of the 2nd and 1st centuries BC similar to those from the Ptolemaic workshops were produced also in the courts of Eastern Hellenistic kings - for example the portrait of Mithridates IV of Pontus (c.159-150 BC), *Geneva* iii, no.219 (see Spier, op.cit. p.35). The Wright gem was acquired in Trebizond which is not very far to the east of the province of Pontus on the Black Sea coast. A number of 3rd century BC bronze rings of Ptolemaic/Hellenistic type with portraits of rulers and deities have also been found in cemeteries in the North Black Sea region. Neverov believes they show evidence of the presence of Egyptian cults in the region from the early Hellenistic period - probably connected with traders and seafarers. He suggests that several of the rings with female portraits may represent Arsinoe III (see O. Neverov, 'A Group of Hellenistic Bronze Rings in the Hermitage', *Vestnik Drevnei Istorii*, 127 (1974), pp.106-115, figs.17-26 and especially figs.19-20 where she wears a *stephane*).

5

Draped bust of a beardless youth or **Apollo**(?) facing to the left against a grille pattern background; his hair runs in fine curved parallel lines from the crown and is gathered in a wide roll round his head with long tightly waved locks; his shoulders are draped and turned to the front.

Black glass cameo bead with three narrow parallel perforations running horizontally across the width; excellent condition with a few small chips round the edge; some small bubbles and striations running vertically on the flat back. (The glass has been tested by XRF and contains manganese and secondary copper, zinc and lead; this is consistent with Ptolemaic glass.)
30 x 23 x 10mm.
Acquired near Mersin (Zephyrion/Hadrianopolis nr Tarsus) on the southern coast of Turkey; given by Mrs Chalfun (ca.1943-5)
2nd or 1st century BC Hellenistic/Ptolemaic

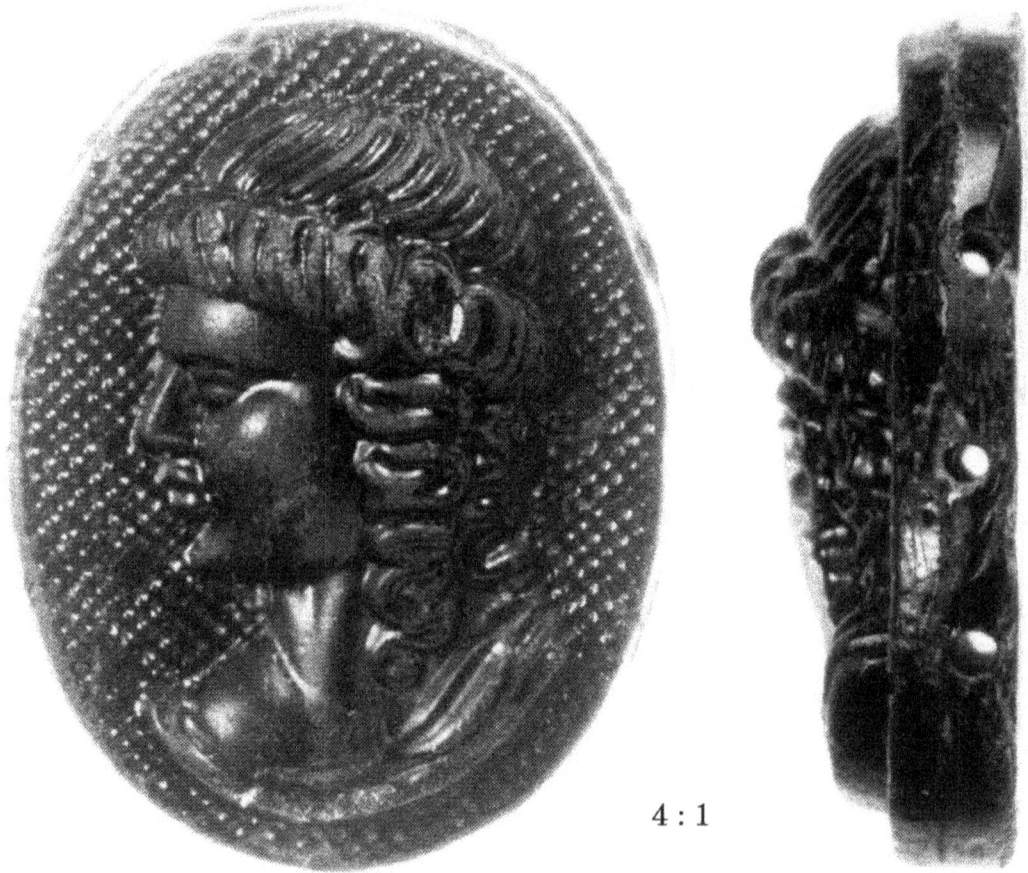

4 : 1

5

This cameo bead seems unusual and no similar examples have come to my notice. The three narrow horizontal perforations suggest that it was used as a spacer bead in a necklace.

The portrait on this cameo could possibly represent a deified Ptolemaic king portrayed as Apollo but, although it somewhat resembles the heads in Spier (op.cit. for 4, nos.37-43, figs 25-7, p.32), he wears no diadem or *stephane* and the treatment of his ringlets is unusual. However, the full smooth, cheek and small pointed chin is characteristic of many Hellenistic portraits.

During the Hellenistic period Mersin (or Zephyrion) seems to have changed hands several times - from Seleucid to Ptolemaic and then back to Seleucid control.

Compare the similar appearance of the heads on the following intagli:
Nuremberg, no.264 - a 'Greek' 2ndc.BC convex cornelian.
Sa'd, no.274 - 2ndc.BC plasma; 'probably a Late Seleucid prince'.

III ROMAN REPUBLICAN & IMPERIAL INTAGLI

6
Zeus/Jupiter wearing a diadem is seated facing in profile to the left on a high-backed throne; his torso is turned in three quarter view to the front and he is draped in a *himation* from the waist down with a panel of drapery hanging from his shoulder; in his left hand he holds a sceptre and in his outstretched right hand he holds out a ***patera*** over a flaming **altar**; behind his throne stands an **eagle** with its head turned back towards him. Ground line.

Chalcedony ringstone with two brown inclusions (like those in moss agate)
17 x 14 x 6 mm. Shape A.4 but with slightly convex sides.
Bought in Bari, May 1946 (?acquired in Zagreb, Croatia; see p.1)
ca. mid 2nd century AD, Roman Imperial

6   4 : 1

This intaglio, like **7**, is related to Kleibrink's 'Imperial small grooves style' of the 1st-2nd century AD (*Hague*, pp.251-2), but it is more carefully engraved than many examples of gems with Zeus enthroned which are often very cursory.

This would have been a popular subject on a soldier's ring but once again seems to be an unusual variation on the Zeus enthroned motif discussed on p.18 (**7**): Zeus (enthroned and with his sceptre) is quite often shown on coins and gems with a *patera*, sometimes held over an eagle (e.g. *BMC Empire V*, pl.72, nos.12,13,19 - coins of Caracalla, 211-217 AD; *Vienna* ii, no.1224ff.). For the symbolism of the eagle see **7** and **28**.

Chalcedony is a popular stone for this motif on gems and it is thought that it might possibly have had a special magic quality (see *Luni*, no.45 with refs.; and also *N.Y.*, no.249, *Cambridge*, nos.253-7, *Vienna* i, nos.398; ii, nos.1224-8 - all chalcedonies).

For other gems showing Zeus holding the *patera* over an altar - though without the eagle behind the throne - see:
Cambridge, no.257 - 2ndc.AD milky chalcedony.
Sa'd, no.10 - 3rdc.AD cornelian; very cursory.
Aquileia, no.17 - flat cornelian (broken in half).
Romania, no.89 - serpentine.

7

In the upper register (a) **Zeus/Jupiter** wearing a diadem is seated facing in profile to the left on a high-backed throne; his torso is turned in three quarter view to the front and he is draped in a *himation* from the waist down; in his left hand he holds a sceptre and in his right outstretched hand a small **Nike/Victory** holding a wreath; at his feet in front of him is an **altar** and behind the throne his **thunderbolt**.
In the lower register (b) an **Eagle between two standards** with its head turned back to the right. Ground line.

Cornelian ringstone, dark reddish-brown; chip on upper left edge.
17 x 13 x 4.5 mm. Shape A.4
Acquired in Belgrade, Yugoslavia (1946).
ca. mid 2nd century AD, Roman Imperial

7   4 : 1

This gem is quite carefully engraved, and detailed with small rounded wheel grooves. Like **6** it is close to Kleibrink's 'Imperial small grooves style' dated 1st-2nd century A.D. (*Hague*, pp.251-2).

Various versions of the motifs in the two registers here (a & b) are quite common, but they usually appear as separate scenes rather than combined on the same intaglio. However, another cornelian gem with similar scenes in two registers shows Zeus seated between the figures of Fortuna and Hermes in the upper register, and the eagle between standards in the lower (*Hanover*, no.1379). These scenes would have been especially popular with soldiers of the Roman army as well as veterans and appear most commonly on gems from the Roman provinces.

(a) *The upper register:* the Zeus enthroned here and on **6** are based on Pheidias' original collosal statue at Olympia which is dated to the third quarter of the 5th century BC. Pheidias used an existing type for his statue and although no copies of the original remain, it has been identified on Roman coins minted between AD 98 and AD 198 as well as on a gem in Paris (Richter 2, no.55; G.M.A. Richter, 'The Pheidian Zeus at Olympia' *Hesperia* 35 (1966) pp.166-170, pl.54). There are many variations on this theme and Zeus can be accompanied by a variety of attributes. He sometimes holds his thunderbolt (e.g. *Hanover*, no.1362) while on this gem it appears in the field behind his throne. The most common version (and the one probably closest to the original statue) shows Zeus holding a Nike or Victory over an eagle standing at his feet (*Vienna* ii, nos.1221-3; *Aquileia*, no.2ff. & p.91; *Dalmatian Gems*, nos.28-9). The throne with reeded (rather than simply turned) legs seems unusual (but cf. Richter 2, no.60).

III Roman Republican & Imperial

Versions of Zeus enthroned appear to be one of the most common subjects on gems from Dalmatia just as they are from Aquileia; about thirty examples are listed in the Split Archaeological Museum gem catalogue compiled by F. Bulić (see *Dalmatian Gems*, nos.28-9).

Zeus holding a Victory over an altar (rather than over the eagle) seems relatively uncommon but another example appears in:
Cambridge, no.252 - a 2ndc.AD cornelian; rather more cursory.

(b) *The lower register:* the eagle was the symbol of Zeus, the Emperor, the legions, the Empire and Imperial victory. The eagle (or the *Aquila*) between legionary standards on gems seems to have been inspired by the motif on coins (e.g. *BMC Republic*, pl.116.2, ca.30 BC) and was obviously connected with the military. It can be combined with a variety of symbols on coins and gems (cf. 28). For the symbolism of the eagle and related examples see *Dalmatian Gems*, nos.261, 263.

For the eagle between standards, see:
Aquileia, no.1281 - convex jasper.
Xanten 1, no.244 -1st-2ndc.AD convex sardonyx.
Sa'd, no.333 - 2ndc.AD convex nicolo (shape C4).
Kibaltchitch, no.82 - dark yellow agate from Olbia; cf. also no.78.
Dreikönigenschreines, no.274 - 1st-2ndc.AD dark cornelian; face slightly convex, back convex; refs.

8

In the centre **Apollo** stands frontally with his head turned in profile to the right; his weight is on his left leg and his right leg is slightly bent; his hair is in a roll round his head and long locks fall down his neck; he has a cloak draped over his right arm and possibly also holds a bow; in his left hand is a *patera*. On the left **Artemis/Diana** stands frontally with her head turned in profile to the right; she wears her short tunic and boots; her hair is swept up and tied on the top of her head; she holds a large flaming torch vertically on her right and in her left hand is a *patera*. Another goddess approaches running in from the right - perhaps **Artemis /Diana** in a different guise or alternatively **Demeter/Ceres, Kore/Persephone/ Proserpina**, or **Hekate**; she wears a long *chiton* with overfold and has her mantle billowing out behind her; her hair is arranged in a roll round her head and falls in long locks down her neck; she holds a short flaming torch in each hand. On either side of the three deities are **two decorated pillars** perhaps representing **Apollo Agyieus** (the aniconic form of Apollo). Ground line.

Red jasper ringstone
16 x 12.5 x 3.5 mm. Shape F.1 (the bevelled edge is slightly irregular). Very good condition.
Acquired in Ordu (Kotyora) on the southern coast of the Black Sea, Turkey (October 1943)
ca.2nd century AD Roman Imperial

8   4 : 1

The details of the minute figures on this gem, all based on Greek statue types, are carefully and accurately engraved with small, rounded wheel grooves for their anatomy and very narrow wheel grooves for drapery, hair etc. This gem is close to the 'Imperial Classicising Style' but also shows characteristics of the 'Imperial Small Grooves style' of the 1st-2nd century AD (*Hague*, pp.194-7, 251-2). Jasper, however, was not used very much for intagli in the 1st century AD but became popular in the 2nd-3rd centuries AD (*Hague*, p.252; *Xanten 2*, pl.XI).

Apollo, and the Artemis in short tunic on the left of this gem, can be identified with certainty but the interpretation of the pillars and the goddess with the two torches on the right is less certain. This goddess (and the corresponding figure on 8x - see below) could represent Artemis in another form or equally well Demeter; offerings were made to Apollo, Artemis and Demeter, who among other functions were divinities of vegetation and fertility. It would have been natural for them to be worshipped together. But in addition to Artemis and Demeter, Kore and Hekate are also shown in this form. The figure-type appears on numerous monuments and coins and, when a torch or torches are the only attributes, these goddesses are indistinguishable from each other. All are inextricably linked with each other and their iconography and functions as earth goddesses overlap (see examples below).

Although the jasper gem was acquired in Ordu (Kotyora), one cannot, of course, be certain of the original provenance. However, if it does have some local significance - perhaps reflecting a local city cult or various cults in Asia Minor - it might be argued from the coin evidence that the figure on the right represents Artemis rather than any of the other goddesses; and if the pillars do represent Apollo Agyieus, then both Apollo and Artemis would appear in two forms on this gem. This would be most unusual - but it would make a pleasingly symmetrical arrangement. The exact identity of the goddess on the right, however, and the significance of the combination of deities shown here must for the moment remain speculative.

The figure types on the intaglio have close parallels on coins, reliefs and other objects, compare:

(1) *Apollo*:
LIMC ii, 'Apollon', no.435a - a 5th century BC bronze statuette in the Ashmolean Museum, Oxford (1971.835) - a very similar Apollo holding a *patera* in his right hand and probably once a bow in his left.
  no.805 - Apollo (with a local god) standing frontally with bow and *patera* on a Hellenistic stele in the Aegina Museum.

Apollo often appears with other gods but especially with Artemis (Diana) with whom he was closely associated; they were brother and sister and were jointly worshipped. They appear frequently alone or together on the Imperial coinage of Asia Minor where the various cults of these deities were particularly popular.

A colony of Ionians from Colophon (near Claros on the Aegean coast of Asia Minor) had been established at Apamea Myrlea (the port for Bursa (Prusa)) on the south coast of the Sea of Marmora (Propontis). This is some distance along the coast to the west of Ordu, but also in the province of Bithynia. The colonists brought with them from their mother-city the famous oracle and ancient cult of Apollo Klarios (or Clarios). On the Imperial coinage of Colophon Apollo Klarios (and Artemis Klaria) are represented by their seated cult statues (see *BMC Ionia*, (Colophon) pp.42-5, nos.47 (with Artemis), 56, 60 - seated cult statue of Apollo Klarios; also nos.44-5, 53 - cult statue of Artemis Klaria).

Both Apollo (as Apollo Klarios) and Artemis (as Diana Lucifer (see under (2a) below)) are identified by legends on the coinage of Apamea. Apollo Klarios, however, is not represented by his usual cult statue but the figure copies a 5th century BC statue type, or types (see *RecGén*, pp.245-6 and p. 246 n.1). The figure-types for both Apollo and Artemis on the coinage of Apamea are the same as those on the intaglio from Ordu.
For Apollo, see:
RecGén, pl.38.9 (p.252, no.40) - Apollo with the legend ΚΛΑΡΙΟΣ ΑΠΟΛΛΩΝ ΜΥΡΛΕΑΝΩΝ on a coin of Claudius (r. AD 41-54); he is shown frontally and with a *patera* just as he appears on the gem. (= *RPC* 1, no.5460 - uncertain mint; Apollo Clarios holding 'phiale(?)'.)
  pl.38.20 (p.254, no.52) - Apollo Clarios on a coin of Marcus Aurelius; but profile view with his left hand is on his hip holding his bow, and *patera* in his right hand.

(2)   (a) *Artemis/Diana*, (b) *Demeter/Ceres*, (c) *Kore/Persephone/Proserpina* or (d) *Hekate* - running with a torch in each hand:
Unless these deities are identified in some way - by a legend or additional attribute (e.g. a crescent moon, an ear of corn etc. (as *Luni*, 85 - Ceres)) - it is impossible to tell one from the other. The examples given below (2a-d) are all close to the running goddess on the gem from Ordu:

(2a) Artemis:
A goddess running with a torch in each hand is a common motif on coins and other objects but seems relatively uncommon on gems:
Munich iii, no.2956 - a convex cornelian-agate of the 2nd-1stc.BC engraved in the Italic-Etruscanising style.
Artemis appears frequently on the coinage of Asia Minor and also of Apamea where she is often, but not always, identified as Diana Lucifer by legends or attributes. See for example:
RecGén, pl.38.18 (p.254, no.48) - Diana Lucifera on a coin of Marcus Aurelius (r. AD 161-180) with the legend DIANAE LVCIF .

(2b) Demeter:
Thorvaldsen, 1717 - 'late Roman cornelian'; the deity standing with a short torch in each hand is identified here as Demeter (?); Fossing compares this figure with the one on the Berlin gem (8x see below) which he states 'cannot be Artemis but is rather to be interpreted as Demeter...'.

This figure type on coins is also often thought to be Demeter (e.g. J. Overbeck, *Greichische Kunstmythologie* ii (Leipzig: 1873-78) Münztafel IX, nos.23-4, 26, p.661) or alternatively, Persephone (see below).

(On the Imperial coinage of Bithynia, Demeter appears frequently but is represented by quite a different figure-type and is easily identifiable: she is almost always shown seated or standing, dressed in a long garment, and with a long torch and holding ears of corn (e.g. *RecGén*, pl.90.9-11 - (Nicomedia) 2ndc.AD).)

(2c) Kore/Persephone/Proserpina:
LIMC viii (Suppl), 'Persephone', no.35 - coin of Cyzikos (in Mysia on the south coast of the Sea of Marmora), Antoninus Pius (r. AD 138-161). This type on coins is often identified as Demeter (see examples for *LIMC* viii, loc.cit., no.35; and (2b) above).

(2d) Hekate:
The representation of Artemis hurrying along with two torches and wearing a long chiton was thought to have been borrowed from Hekate and so she sometimes appears as her double. They were often worshipped together (Farnell, *Cults* 2, pp.505-6, 516) and Hekate also seems to have been popular on the coast and interior of Asia Minor. Her cult was probably of Thracian origin and perhaps had connections with the Black Sea (see Farnell, *Cults* 2, ch.13 & 16; and *LIMC* vi (addenda) 'Hekate', no.65ff. - Hekate or Artemis).

(This multi-purpose figure appears also on a rare coin of Gallienus, probably from Syria or Turkey, with the legend ABVNDANTIA AVG dated ca.AD 267-8. (Paris (BN) inv.288/1975).)

(3) *Artemis/Diana* in short tunic and holding a large torch:
This standing type of Artemis seems less common on coins and gems where the hunting type of Artemis, often running, is usually shown with her bow and quiver (e.g. *RecGén*, pl.70.15 - a Bithynian coin of Marcus Aurelius). However, the type with large torch does appear on other objects, compare:
LIMC ii, 'Apollon/Apollo', no.360 - Artemis (with Apollo) wearing her short tunic and holding a long torch (like the figure on the left of the gem) on a 3rd century AD votive relief in the Capitoline Museum, Rome (*BullCom* 1889, 221 pl.9).
LIMC ii, 'Artemis', no.988 - a 1st century BC terracotta statuette from Myrina in Asia Minor (Paris, Louvre, Myr 198 (190)).

(4) *The Pillars: Apollo Agyieus(?)*:
Pillars sometimes appear on gems in ritual or offering scenes, but these are rather different. Compare for example:
Dalmatian Gems, no.180 - a 1stc.BC - 1stc.AD cornelian; a similar symmetrical arrangement of figures and pillars as on the Ordu gem: in the centre an image of Dionysos with a female figure on either side (one dancing, one playing a flute); plain pillars on either side - one surmounted with an urn, the other an image of Priapus.

The isolated pillars on the Ordu gem do not seem to be architectural. Horizontal bands of decoration are clearly visible and pillars, sometimes decorated, can represent Apollo in his very early aniconic form. Although the pillars of Apollo Agyieus were usually conical, other types are attested. Compare:
LIMC ii, 'Apollon Agyieus', no.8 - a truncated pillar of Apollo Agyieus with inscription (Corfu Mus.). Rhomaios suggests that this is a combination of the pointed conical type and the altar type of Agyieus and could have had a concave area at the top to receive offerings (see C.A. Rhomaios, 'Les premières fouilles de Corfou' in *BCH* 49 (1925) pp.211-18; Rhomaios also suggests (op.cit., p.217) that this pillar marked the boundary of a sanctuary of Apollo near a

III Roman Republican & Imperial

temple of Artemis); see discussion in *LIMC* ii, 'Apollon Agyieus', p.331 especially; and Farnell, *Cults* 4, pp.307-8).

no.4 - 3rdc.BC Greek coin of Byzantium (Thrace) with Agyieus column reflecting the city's cult of Apollo (= E. Schönert-Geiss, *Die Münzprägung von Byzantion*, i (1970), nos.1215 & 1232).

nos.2-3, 5-6 - Greek coins of 4th-1stc. BC with Agyieus column; compare with Schönert-Geiss, op.cit., ii (1972) pl.114, nos.1898-9 - late 1stc.BC coins, 'Apollo/Obelisk series', p.131 (= *RPC* 1, no.1773).

no.27 - two 1stc.AD funerary pillars, but with their tops missing (Museo Civico, Padova, no.253). The bulbous shape of these pillars with their horizontal bands of decoration resemble those on the Ordu gem.

Apollo was among his many roles regarded as the protector of migrating tribes and the deity of colonisation. The Apollo Agyieus pillars were also supposed to have marked certain stations on the Sacred Way during the migrations from the north and so it would have been fitting for him to have also been worshipped in this form in a colony on the Black Sea (as he was in Byzantium). Apollo Agyieus belonged to both public and private cult and the pillars were placed at the entrances to houses as well as on roads. Apollo was the protector of streets and, like Artemis and Selene (who was identified with both Artemis and Hekate) he filled the roads with light (see Farnell, *Cults* 4, pp.148-51, 307ff.).

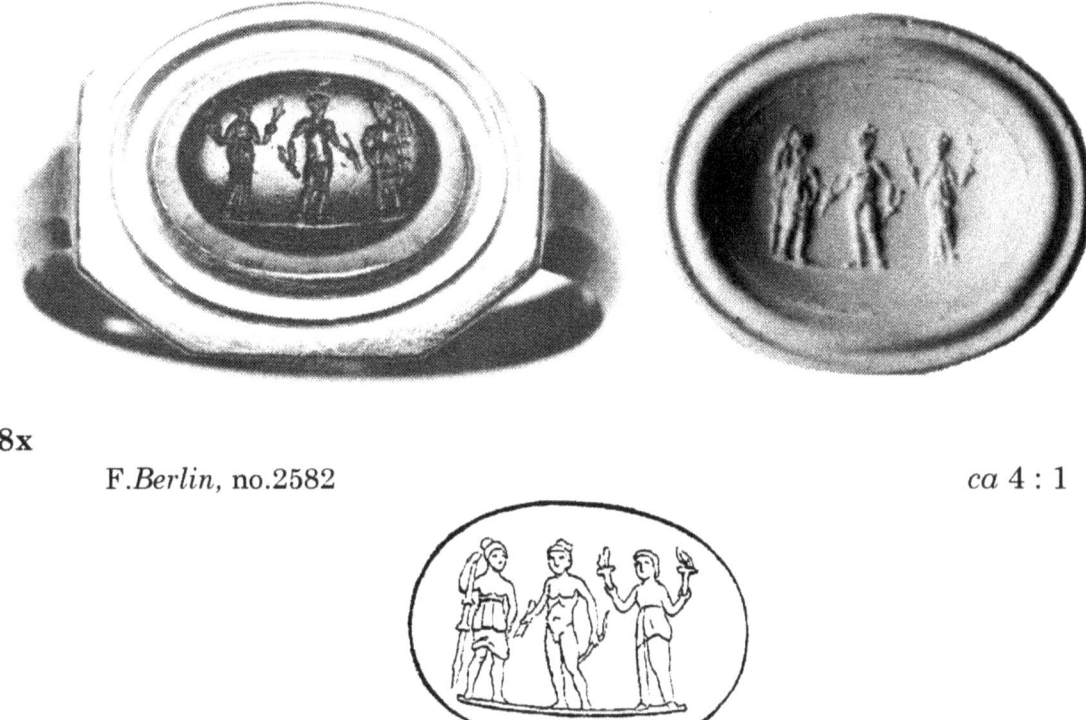

8x

F.*Berlin*, no.2582   ca 4 : 1

A Roman intaglio, once in the collection of Baron Philipp von Stosch and later acquired by Frederick the Great in 1764, is now in the Antikensammlung, Berlin (**8x**). The motif on this intaglio is very similar to the one on the gem from Ordu and, although there are no pillars, it may show the same three deities. A different figure-type, however, has been used for the goddess standing on the right. See:

F.*Berlin*, no.2582 (= C. O. Müller & F. Wieseler, *Denkmäler der Alten Kunst*, ii (Leipzig:1899) pl.XXV, 6 (see line drawing **8x**), refs. p.306; & Overbeck, op.cit., Gemmentafel IV no.9 (8), p.507) - a three-layered convex sardonyx with a brown upper layer and opaque white crackled layer below which indicates heating. The gem is carefully worked with very small drills and Dr G. Platz dates this gem to the second half of the 1st century AD (personal communication).

The Apollo standing in the centre holding his bow, and the Artemis in short tunic on the left here are close to the corresponding figures on the Ordu gem, but the enigmatic goddess on the right in a long *chiton*, holding up a torch in either hand, stands frontally with her left leg bent. The identity of this figure seems uncertain and she also could represent any of the goddesses suggested for the running deity with two torches on the Ordu gem (see (2a-d) above).

The Berlin version of the goddess with two torches also appears (though less frequently than the running type) on the 3rd century AD Imperial coinage of Nicomedia (Bithynia) where she is thought to represent Artemis Phosphoros - although this identification is not supported by a legend or further attributes (see *RecGén*, pl.96.10, pl.97.23, pl.98.34). (A veiled version is sometimes identified as Demeter (op.cit., pl.90.8 - 2ndc.AD; Nicomedia)). However, an Artemis of this type (identified by the deer beside her), but wearing a short tunic, appears on a relief from Thrace (*LIMC* ii, 'Artemis (in Thracia)', no.17 - 2nd-3rdc.AD).

The identity of the goddess on the Berlin gem has been discussed several times in the past: Fossing (*Thorvaldsen*, no.1717, p.232 - see 2b above) and Overbeck identify her as Demeter, while Furtwängler and Müller identify her as Hekate(?) who is sometimes shown like this (op.cit. under 8x p.23). Fossing remarks that three-figure groups of deities are characteristic of later Imperial gems and that they recall the similarly composed votive reliefs set up by soldiers on the Esquiline in the 3rd century AD (*Thorvaldsen*, no.1657, refs.).

It is possible that the three deities on both these gems might have been copied from a relief or some other object and perhaps reflect a local cult or cults from Asia Minor. But for the moment the identity of the goddesses with two torches on the right of both the Ordu and the Berlin gem - as well as the significance of the two pillars on the former - must remain uncertain.

9
Artemis/Diana stands frontally with her head in profile to the left; she is wearing a long *peplos* with overfold and a panel of drapery flutters out below her left elbow; her weight is on her right leg and her left leg is slightly bent; she holds out her bow (partly obscured by the chip) in her right hand and raises her left arm to take an arrow from the quiver over her left shoulder.   Ground line.

Garnet ringstone, dark red translucent (contains iron and manganese; tested by XRF); a large chip on the right edge.
9.5 x ca.7 x 2.5 mm overall; face 9 x ca.6 mm.   Shape F.2 (very slightly convex face)
Acquired in Giresun (Cerasus) on the southern coast of the Black Sea, Turkey (December 1941)
1st or 2nd century AD Roman Imperial

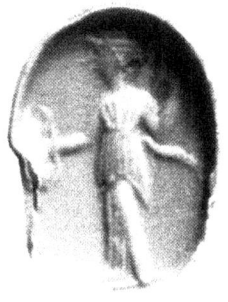

9   4 : 1

This small intaglio is in the Imperial Classicising Style (*Hague*, pp.196-7) but the treatment of the facial features relates it also to Kleibrink's 'Chin-mouth-nose style' of the 1st-2nd century AD (*Hague*, p.294). Details of drapery are carefully engraved with narrow wheel grooves.

This type of Artemis is derived from an original Greek statue of ca.370-330 BC which survives in Roman copies (see *LIMC* ii, 'Artemis', nos.129-33 - the 'Beirut-Venice Artemis'; esp. no.133 a 2nd century AD copy at Holkham Hall, Norfolk; and compare also no.1131 the relief on the base of a thymiaterion or candalabra of the imperial period from Delos (Marseille, Mus. Borély 1585)). A few Hellenistic gems illustrate the type (see especially Plantzos, *Hellenistic*, no.286 below). On gems of the Roman period, however, this type of Artemis seems much less common than the type wearing short tunic and boots (cf. 8) often running and usually accompanied by her hounds.

For related examples, see:
Plantzos, *Hellenistic*, no.286, p.77 (= F.*Berlin*, no.1042; *LIMC* ii, 'Artemis', no.135) - 2ndc.BC Hellenistic long oval, convex cornelian from Lemessos in Cyprus; slender Artemis in high girt *peplos*; this Roman intaglio from Giresun is clearly closely modelled on this type.
Munich i, no.348 (= *LIMC* ii, loc.cit. no.134) - 3rd-2ndc.BC cornelian; the figure is reversed and her head faces the other way.
Munich iii, no.3129 - imperial glass paste; Diana seen more in profile.
Vienna ii, no.1454 - a 3rd-4thc.AD cornelian; a very cursory example.

10

Hermes/Mercury, naked apart from the cloak (*chlamys*) draped over his right arm, faces in profile to the right with his torso turned in three quarter view to the front and his left leg raised on a sphere or boulder; he rests his elbow on his raised left knee and cups his chin in his hand; he wears his winged cap (*petasus*) and his hair is in a roll round his head; he holds his winged *caduceus* behind him. Ground line.

Garnet ringstone, pinkish-red (tested by XRF); rutile needles are visible inside the stone (var. almandine?); set in a modern (19th or 20th century?) gold ring.
ca.11 x 8 x ? (h.8 mm bezel and stone). Shape C8 (highly convex face and concave back).
Setting: h.26 x diam. of hoop 19 mm; the bezel is open behind; the shoulders are stepped and the bezel is in three sections which are separated by horizontal pierced grooves: the hoop and shoulder are attached to the central band by small struts at four points, and this central band is in turn soldered to the collar holding the stone at four more points hidden underneath. Modern (19th or 20th century)?
Unknown provenance
Second half of the 1st century BC - first half of 1st century AD Roman Republican

10
4 : 1

3 : 1

Small round drill holes have been used for the detailing of anatomy - especially on the feet and arms which relates this gem to Kleibrink's 'Republican Extinguishing Pellet style' dated to the second half of the 1st century BC - first half of the 1st century AD (*Hague*, p.145).

There are numerous figures of different gods, warriors and heroes shown in various positions with one foot raised on a sphere, stone or other object (e.g. *Dalmatian Gems*, nos.162-6). It has been suggested that the basic type was derived from a Greek statue of the 4th century BC by Lysippus (see Richter 2, no.66, p.30; but Horster rejects the theory: *Statuen* - 'Hermes-Achill', pp.29-32, pl.7.1-4). Different figure-types are often combined and they carry or wear attributes belonging to other deities (e.g. *Thorvaldsen*, no.574 = *LIMC vi*, 'Mercurius', no.124(a) - an early Augustan sardonyx, Poseidon/Mercury).

A number of intagli are quite close to this gem but show slight variations: when Mercury holds *caduceus* behind him, he usually then holds his money bag out in front (e.g. *Munich* iii, no.2519 - 3rdc.AD cornelian) or when his *caduceus* is held in front of him, he has his hand behind his back (e.g. *Berlin*, no.363 = *LIMC* vi, 'Mercurius', no.154 - 1stc. B.C. cornelian; *Xanten* 2, no.9 - 1stc.AD cornelian; Horster, *Statuen*, pl.7.1).

The Mercury on this gem with his chin resting on his hand seems a less usual variation on the types discussed above, but compare:

Naples i, no.72 - banded agate with flat face, convex back, from Herculaneum; a cursorily engraved gem with the figure uncertainly identified as Hermes(?); he rests his elbow on his knee and has his hand raised towards his chin but the *caduceus*(?) behind him is unclear; his pose, however, is very close to the one on the Wright garnet where the *caduceus* is clear and this suggests that the Herculaneum gem also represents Hermes/ Mercury.

F.*Berlin*, no.7624 - an Imperial flat, white banded sard; a related type showing a hero with his foot raised on a helmet and his hand raised towards his chin.

11

Hermes/Mercury stands naked in profile to the left with his torso turned to the front; his right leg is flexed with his heel raised off the ground and his weight is on his left leg; he holds his *caduceus* on his left and has his cloak (*chlamys*) draped over his arm; in his right hand he holds out his money bag and at his feet stands a cock (or ram?). Ground line.

Cornelian ringstone, dark reddish-brown; slight scratching on the face and a small chip on the left edge; set in a modern gold ring
ca.11 x 8 x 4 mm. Shape A1 (convex face and back)
Setting: h.21 x diam. of hoop 19.5 mm
Acquired near Sadak (Satala), Cappadocia, eastern Turkey (June 1942)
1st century AD Roman Imperial

11   4 : 1

This gem is engraved in a rather similar style to **10** but there is less use of pelleting for details which relates it more to the Classicising style of the 1st century AD.

Mercury standing with purse and *caduceus* is one of the most common subjects on intagli in the Roman era and probably reproduces a Roman cult statue. Sena Chiesa suggests that Mercury holding the money bag may have been the type adopted by the Collegia Mercatorum (see *Aquileia*, pp.137-8 for an account and lists of examples on gems, metal work and other objects).

This is a finer example than many and can be dated slightly earlier than gems which belong to the usual cursory series (e.g. *Dalmatian Gems*, no.58; *Exeter*, nos.56-7; *Erimtan*, nos.63-9 - mostly 2ndc.AD); careful attention has been paid to the modelling of his torso with small rounded wheel grooves. On the Wright intaglio Mercury's neo-classical stance is closer to Praxitelean prototypes and the figure still shows the influence of late Hellenistic models. However, Mercury has already acquired his money bag, an attribute which was to become so usual on later Roman Imperial gems (*Luni*, no.25, pp.62-3). One of Mercury's animal attributes - either the cock or the ram - stands at his feet in front (cf. *Munich* ii, nos.1198-1202 (= *LIMC* vi, 'Mercurius', no.110) - second half of the 1stc.BC Italic glass pastes; *Aquileia*, no.188ff.).

Mercury standing with *caduceus* and money bag is almost always seen frontally (e.g. *Exeter*, no.37 - early 1stc.AD cornelian; and *Erimtan*, nos.63-69 - mostly 2ndc.AD) and this usual frontal type also appears on 2nd century AD coins of Prusius ad Hippium in Bithynia (*RecGén*, pl.104.25 - Lucius Verus).

The figure on this gem, however, in neo-classical pose reflecting earlier models is less usual, but compare:
Kassel, no.60 (=*LIMC* vi, 'Mercurius' no.117) - a 1stc.AD nicolo; a close parallel where Mercury adopts the same stance and holds the same type of money bag (refs.).
Luni, no.25 - end 1stc.BC flat red cornelian; a similar type to the above (refs.)

12
Ares/Mars stands facing to the front with his head turned in profile to the left; his weight is on his right leg and his left leg is bent; he wears his plumed helmet and boots and has his cloak draped across his torso and over his left arm; on his left is his sword and his large round shield with central boss; his spear stands on his right. Ground line.

Cornelian ringstone, orange; very good condition.
16 x 12.5 x 4mm. Shape F.1/A.4 (very slightly convex face)
Acquired in Silifke (Seleucia) on the southern coast of Turkey (June 1943)
1st-2nd century AD Roman Imperial

12   4 : 1

The figure is engraved rather cursorily with large rounded wheel-drill grooves without internal detailing. The head is drawn with a single wide vertical groove and the chin, mouth and nose are added with short, fine wheel grooves. Narrower drills are used for other details. This is close to Kleibrink's 'Round Head style' dated 1st-2nd century AD which is related to the earlier 'Imperial Wheel' and 'Flat Bouterolle styles' (*Hague*, pp.179, 285). These styles are close to Zwierlein-Diehl's 'Flachperlstil' (see *Hague*, loc.cit., and *Snettisham*, p.26).

This nude type of Mars seems close to Hellenistic models (for earlier versions of the motif, see *Vienna* i, no.114 - 2ndc.BC Hellenistic; ii, no.1095 - beginning of the 1stc.BC). The more usual figure of Mars on Roman gems is shown in his legionary uniform - a type probably copied from a contemporary cult statue (cf. *Xanten* 1, no.154; *Luni*, no.61, and remarks p.83).

For similar figures, compare:
Xanten 1, no.115 - end 1st - first half of 2ndc.AD nicolo; naked, no sword.
   no.154a - 1st-2ndc.AD flat sard (mid brown); motif and style close to this gem from Silifke (Seleucia) but here Mars is without his shield.
Dreikönigenschreines, no.72 - second half of the 1stc.AD flat cornelian (F.1); a very similar Mars in the 'Flachperlstil' but he faces to the right and his shield is on the ground.

13
Aphrodite/Venus Victrix is seen in three quarter view from behind with her head in profile to the right and her left elbow resting on a pillar; her weight is on her left leg and her right one is bent; she is naked apart from the mantle draped round her legs; her hair is gathered in a roll round her head and she wears a diadem knotted at the back; she holds a plumed helmet out before her in her right hand and holds a spear and palm branch diagonally on her left; her round shield, decorated with rays round a central boss, is propped against the pillar behind her. Ground line.

Plasma ringstone, moss green; slight scratching on face.
12 x 9 x 4mm. Shape A.4
Unknown provenance (bought at Petworth 1953)
End of the 1st - 2nd century AD Roman Imperial

13   4 : 1

This Venus Victrix belongs to the Imperial Classicising style dated from the time of Augustus to the early 2nd century AD (*Hague*, p.194ff. and no.529ff.). Details of the head and anatomy are quite carefully engraved on this intaglio. (For small plasma gems see also **23** and **36**.)

Versions of Venus Victrix are common and often engraved on small, convex plasma gems like this which date mostly to the 1st century AD (*Vienna* ii, iii, nos.1460ff., 2801-03 (refs.); *Dreikönigenschreines*, no.225; *LIMC* viii, 'Venus Victrix', p.211; *Dalmatian Gems*, no.64ff.). The type is probably derived from a Hellenistic statue of the 4th-3rd century BC. In 29 BC, a three quarter back-view version of Venus Victrix appeared on the coinage of Octavian (*BMC Empire* i, pl.14.16-17 = *LIMC* viii, loc. cit., no.198). The decoration on the shield which appears on a number of gems refers to the *Sidus Iulium* - the star which appears on Augustan coins (e.g. *Vienna* ii, no.1465, *Nuremberg*, no.210 - a 2ndc.AD slightly convex cornelian engraved in very similar style). Julius Caesar was believed to have had Venus Victrix engraved on his seal and a frontal version of the goddess appeared on his coinage in 45-44 BC.

Venus shown in back view leaning on a column, often with a shield on the ground beside her and carrying a spear and helmet - the arms of her lover Mars - was to become the most usual figure type of the goddess on coins and intagli. Less often she is shown with a palm frond over her shoulder and an apple or a globe on her outstretched hand (*Aquileia*, nos.262-4, pp.158-60; *Vienna* ii no.1478a - 2nd-3rdc.AD plasma (= *LIMC* viii, loc.cit., no.206), & no.1480; *Nuremberg*, no.212; *Dalmatian Gems*, no.66; *Cambridge*, no.292, see below).

This gem is unusual as it combines attributes from both these iconographic types, the warlike and victorious. It appears related to a coin type of Julia Domna, AD 198-209, where Venus (although seen from the front) leans on a column with the shield at her feet, and carries the helmet and palm - but no spear (*BMC Empire* v, pl.29.2).

No exact parallel has come to my notice but a few other intagli also show mixed iconography or variations on the usual types:

Munich iii, no.2491 - 2nd-3rdc.AD flat lapis lazuli; Venus stands in frontal view as on the coin described above; she also holds a palm frond and helmet but here she is accompanied by two cupids - one with a helmet, the other with an apple - symbolising again her warlike and victorious roles.

Vienna ii, no.1477 - 2nd-3rdc.AD red jasper; Venus with apple and spear.

Cambridge, no.292 - (?) 1stc.AD olive green plasma; Venus Victrix seen as usual from behind holding an apple - but with a dove perched on the palm; and so the shield is her only warlike attribute here.

14
Eros/Cupid stands in profile to the right with his weight on his right leg and his left one slightly bent with his heel raised off the ground; a mantle is draped over his shoulder with the ends falling behind him and in front; he holds a bird (a dove?) out in his right hand. Ground line.

Plasma ringstone, yellowish green with a few dark inclusions; some slight scratches on the face.
14 x 12 x 4mm. Shape F.1/A.4 (very slightly convex face)
Acquired in Istanbul (Byzantium, Constantinople), Turkey (given by Guy Thompson 1942)
1st century BC Roman Republican

14   4 : 1

This gem belongs to Kleibrink's 'Italic-Republican Pellet style' dated 2nd -1st century BC (*Hague*, pp.131-2, and compare the Cupids nos.206-8). The small round bouterolle drill has been used to mark the features, hairstyle, joints, the tips of wings, ends of drapery etc. and produces the characteristic small round holes (or 'pelleting') in the intaglio.

Eros (Cupid) is often shown engaging in a variety of activities and sometimes he borrows the attributes of other deities. Here he holds a bird - perhaps the dove, an attribute of his mother, Aphrodite (see *Cambridge*, no.84 - a Hellenistic cornelian; and no.292 - see under **13**). For this chubby type of Cupid with small wings, see remarks for **15**.

This motif on gems is unusual, but compare:
Munich iii, no. 3429 - glass paste, opaque green with blue and white streak; Eros in an *aedicula*, but standing in the same position and also holding a dove.
F.*Berlin*, no.938 - Eros stands in an *aedicula*, as above, but without the dove.
   no.943 - an Italic sardonyx intaglio; Eros is engraved in similar style; he holds up a helmet (an attribute of Mars and also Venus, cf. **13**).

15
Eros/Cupid walks in profile to the right with his bow raised to shoot an arrow. Ground line.

Nicolo ringstone, blue on black; fine condition; set in modern gold ring.
10 x 8mm overall; face 8 x 5mm. Shape F.4 (?)
Ring h.20 x diam. of hoop 16mm.
Bought in Bari, May 1946 (?acquired in Zagreb, Croatia; see p.1)
2nd century AD Roman Imperial

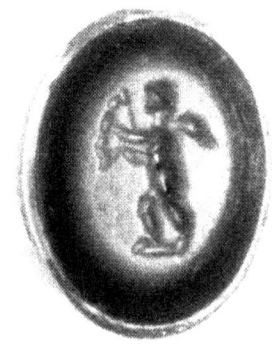
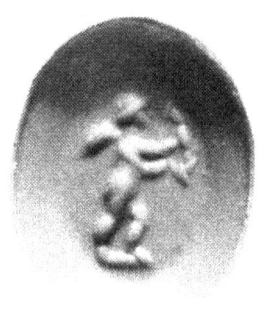

15   4 : 1

This intaglio belongs to the 'Imperial Plain Grooves style' dated 1st-3rd century AD (*Hague*, p.311). This was a popular style for nicolos where the minute figures are engraved with thick, rounded wheel grooves which go through to the dark layer of the stone so that the motifs stand out clearly against the lighter upper layer. The stones usually have bevelled obverse edges which suggests that they probably protruded from the bezel of the ring - a type of setting which is characteristic of finger rings from the 2nd century AD onwards.

Eros with bow and arrow was a popular motif in the Classical period where he is shown as a slender youth with large wings (e.g. *GGFR*, pl.633 (= *F.Berlin*, no.351; *LIMC* iii, 'Eros', no.343) - a 4thc.BC Classical Greek cornelian, signed 'Olympios'). This type continues into the Imperial period, sometimes on glass pastes (e.g. *Vienna* ii, no.615 (= *LIMC* iii, 'Eros/Amor, Cupido', no.141) - 1stc.AD glass paste; *Hanover*, no.804). However, in the 1st century BC, and especially during the Augustan period, the younger, chubby type of Cupid with small wings became popular. This type was to become usual in the Roman period.

On Roman intagli the motif of Cupid shooting an arrow from his bow is relatively uncommon but there are a number of examples with the chubby, small-winged type of Cupid, compare:
Plantzos, *Hellenistic*, no.526 (= *F.Berlin* no.1115) - 1stc.BC Greco-Roman convex garnet.
Hanover, no.134 - first half of 1stc.BC convex chalcedony; refs.
Britain, no.135 - 1stc.AD small convex plasma from Richborough.
Gaul, no.364 - 50 BC - A.D.50 convex plasma in an ancient ring; from Nîmes.
Romania, no.180 - grey sardonyx in similar style.
Bari, no.55 - 3rdc.AD cornelian (shape F.1).
Aquileia, no.306 - convex cornelian; refs. to the type on other objects, p.171.

16
Eros/Cupid is seated on a pile of rocks facing in profile to the right playing the double flute or *tibiae*. Ground line.

Red jasper ringstone; set in modern gold ring with the bezel filled in at the back.
12 x 9 x ca.2mm; flat face. Shape F.1 (?)
Ring h.23 x diam. of hoop 22mm.
Acquired in Ohrid, Macedonia (October 1946)
ca.2nd century AD Roman Imperial

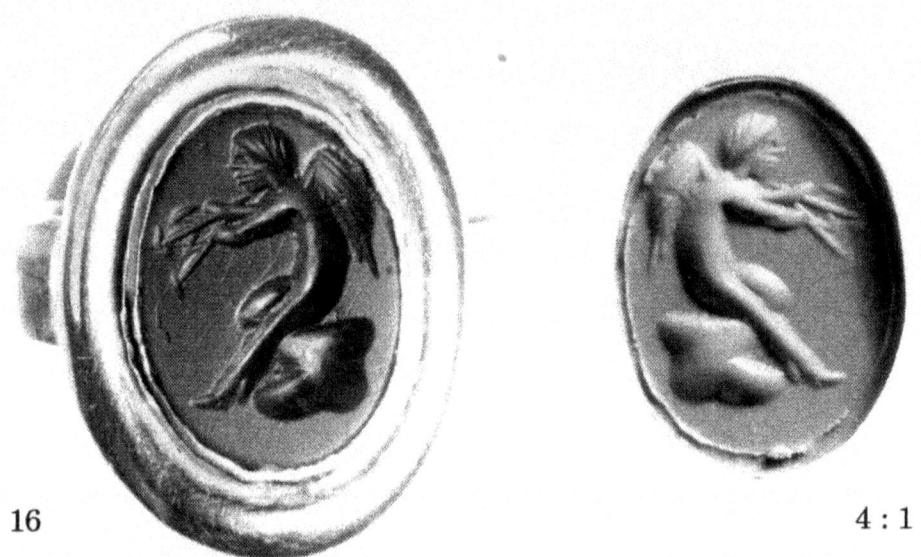

16   4 : 1

The engraving of this jasper shows characteristics of the 'Imperial Transitional styles' and especially the 'Imperial Chin-mouth-nose style' dated 1st-2nd century AD (*Hague*, p.251ff., p.294). In some respects this style appears to be a simplified continuation of the 'Republican Wheel style' (cf. **18**). Cupid's facial features are engraved with several horizontal grooves and his hair, in a stylised roll round the head, is detailed with short grooves. His body is drawn with a single sweep of a broad, rounded drill (cf. the seated satyr engraved in very similar style, *Hanover*, no.1482 - a red jasper dated 2nd-3rdc.AD; for red jasper intagli see *Hague*, p.252 and also *Xanten* 2, pl.XI).

An early example of the motif appears on a Greco-Persian chalcedony scaraboid of the 4th century BC - two erotes, one playing the lyre and the other the *tibiae*, are shown seated on rocks facing each other (*GGFR*, no.951). In Roman art Cupid is often shown as a musician - see R. Stuveras, *Le Putto dans l'art romain*, Collection Latomus 99 (Brussels: 1969) p.104. Satyrs are also shown seated playing the double flute and a number of examples come from Gaul (cf. especially *Gaul*, nos.290-1). For the double flute see M. Henig, 'A Roman Intaglio from Chichester', *Ant.Jnl.* (1978) pp.374-7, and especially A. Wardle, 'A Note on the *Tibiae*', *ibid.* pp.376-7, pl.76 - a plasma gem with seated Marsyas playing the *tibiae*.

Cupid is quite often shown playing the flute, but usually walking or standing. He is seldom shown seated, but there are a few examples including another one from Dalmatia:
Exeter, no.38 - 1st-2nd century AD flat, red jasper engraved in a rather different style ('Imperial Classicising style') from Epidaurum (ex.coll. Sir Arthur Evans); the same scene though Cupid sits under a tree; (see further refs.).
Madrid, no.255 - a 2ndc.AD flat, red jasper; here Cupid, engraved in very similar style, is seated on the ground playing his flute.

17
A naked **Satyr** sitting on a low stone seat in profile to the right leans forward to contemplate an animal's head (an antelope's?) held out in his right hand; his *thyrsos* appears behind his left shoulder. Ground line (?)

Cornelian ringstone, orange; very small scratches on surface.
13 x 12 x 5mm. Shape F.1 (very slightly convex face)
Acquired in Silifke (Seleucia) on the southern coast of Turkey (June 1943)
1st century BC - AD 30 Roman Republican

17   4 : 1

The round shape and the engraving style of this gem is typical of the 'Republican Wheel style' dated 1st century BC -AD 30 (*Hague*, pp.154-5). Rather short, wide grooves of varying thicknesses running in different directions are used for the anatomy, and narrower grooves for details. The engraving of the head is also typical - his hair is in a roll round his head and stylised so that it looks like a hat with a rim. Gems with Dionysiac subjects (like this example) were often engraved in the wheel style and many come from Aquileia (cf. the treatment of the satyrs' anatomy *Hague*, nos.335, 337 etc.; *Erimtan*, no.43 - Pan; *Dreikönigenschreines*, no.93 - slightly convex cornelian (shape A.5) dated second half of the 1st century BC; linear style but by the same hand as *Hague*, no.335).

There are many variations on the seated satyr motif on gems and coins. A satyr holding a *syrinx* and *pedum* but seated on a rock in the same position as on the gem appears on a coin of the 2nd century AD minted in Bithynia (*RecGén*, pl.53.23 - Antoninus Pius (Cretia Flaviopolis)).

Satyrs often hold masks but the satyr on this gem appears to hold an antelope's head; compare especially:
Vienna i, no.244 - 1st century BC slightly convex cornelian; seated satyr with mask; same posture and type.

18

A naked **Satyr** dancing on tip-toe towards the left holds out a bunch of grapes in his right hand; he has a goat-skin (*nebris*) draped over his left arm and part of his throwing-stick (*logobolon*) is just visible by the chip on the edge of the stone. Ground line.

Cornelian ringstone, dark reddish-brown with black inclusions (tested by XRF); matte surface and a chip on the upper left edge.
13 x 10 x 3mm. Shape F.1 with very slightly convex back.
Acquired in Aleppo (Beroea), Syria (1943)
ca.2nd century AD Roman Imperial

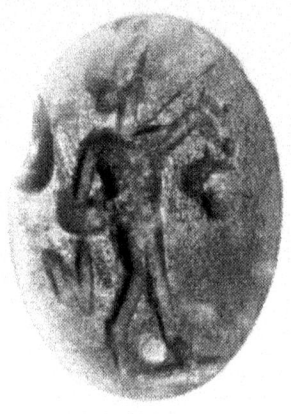 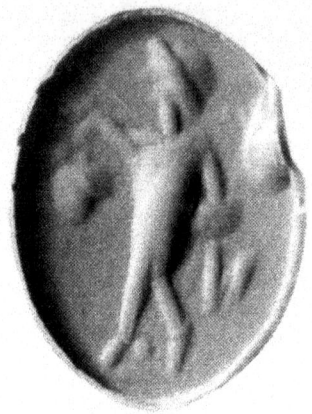

18   4 : 1

The surface of this gem is worn but it seems cursorily engraved with little internal detailing. The satyr resembles some of the figures engraved in Kleibrink's 'Imperial Plain or Incoherent Grooves style' dated 1st-3rd and 3rd century AD (*Hague*, pp.311, 326; and cf. no.1038).

The motif is common on gems and other objects (see *Aquileia*, pp.188-9). Satyrs, as followers and servants of Bacchus/Dionysos, were associated with drink and good living and so were popular subjects for soldiers' rings (see also **17**). These satyrs usually dance to the right (in impression) but on this intaglio and on several of the examples listed below they dance to the left which is unusual.

Similar examples have turned up all over the empire. One hundred and seventeen cornelian intagli were found in a Roman jeweller's hoard discovered at Snettisham and these can be securely dated to the 2nd century AD. The hand of three different gem engravers can be recognised among them (see Kleibrink in *Snettisham*, p.25ff.). Five of the intagli are engraved with satyrs, and one example (see below) is quite close to this gem from Aleppo. Compare the following examples and lists provided:

Snettisham, no.233 - 2ndc.AD cornelian set in a ring; a satyr with grapes, *nebris* and *logobolon* engraved in similar style to the Aleppo example - but dancing to the right in impression (p.98); also nos.181-2, 226-7.
Britain, nos.159-77, esp.no.161 - cornelian with black inclusions.
Caerleon, no.64 - red jasper dated AD 160-230; the satyr also dances to the left.
Nuremberg, no.58 - 2nd-3rdc.AD flat red jasper; again the satyr dances to the left.
 no.57 - 2ndc.AD flat red jasper; in very similar style to the Aleppo gem, but here he holds a hare.
Gaul, nos.255-72 - several examples are in a similar cursory style.
Aquileia, nos.390-1 - an agate and a cornelian; also nos.393-8.
Vienna ii, no.1393 - 3rd-4thc.AD jasper in similar style.
Exeter, no.58 - 3rdc.AD nicolo from Seaton Roman villa (Devon).
Romania, no.251 - red jasper; a good parallel.

19

Silenus head (or mask) turned very slightly to the right; he has a long wispy beard, a round nose and prominent cheek bones; the leaves and fronds of an ivy wreath cover his ears and fall down on either side of his bald head.

Cornelian ringstone, orange; fine condition with a high polish
10 x 8 x 3mm.   Shape F.1
Acquired in Silifke (Seleucia) on the southern coast of Turkey (June 1943)
Second half of the 1st century BC Roman Republican

19   4 : 1

A very skilfully engraved fine quality 'Greco-Roman' gem. The different planes of the Silenus' face and details of the head are carefully and accurately shown on this minute gem. The image is deeply engraved so that in the impression it appears in high relief. There are quite a number of Silenus masks, often in glass paste (e.g. *Hanover,* nos.498-500 - all second half of the 1stc.BC; nos.613-5 - second half of the 1stc.BC). The types vary and some are more mask-like than others. This example appears more naturalistic than many and resembles heads found on sculpture and terracottas.

For comparable examples, but mostly more mask-like and stylised, see:
Plantzos, *Hellenistic,* no.566 (= F.*Berlin,* no.1108) - a naturalistic Silenus bust on a 1st century BC
    Greco-Roman convex garnet.
Geneva, no.335 - mid 1stc.BC flat layered sardonyx; a gem of similar quality; (refs. p.311)
Dalmatian Gems, no.106 - an Evans sealing of a nicolo from Salona, 1stc.BC - 1stc.AD.
Vienna i, nos.329-330 - flat cornelians of the second to third quarter of the 1stc.BC; similar but
    more stylised.
Thorvaldsen, nos.1244, 1247 - a Greco-Roman nicolo and a yellow glass paste.

20
Bust of a **Maenad** facing in profile to the left with her lips slightly parted; she has a wreath of ivy leaves and berries round her head; her hair is gathered in a bun at the nape of her neck and long wavy locks fall over her shoulders; a few folds of her *chiton* are just visible beneath her left shoulder and breast, and she carries her *thyrsos* over her right shoulder.

Gold ruby glass ringstone (tested by XRF; and SEM with EDXA system).
15 x 12 x 3.5mm. Shape F.7; the back is irregular and seems to have been finished off by hand.
Unknown provenance (bought at Petworth 1953)
An 18th century or later copy of an original intaglio in the Neo-Attic tradition of the second quarter of the 1st century BC

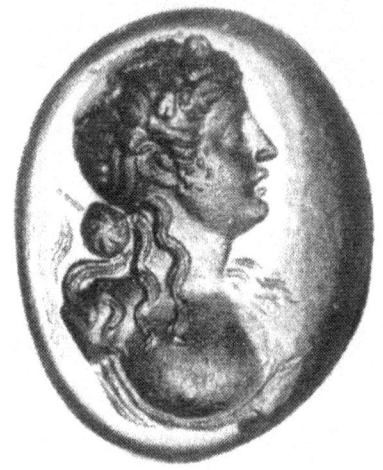 

20 4 : 1

This red paste gem has been tested and appears to be a potash-lead-silica glass. It is very low in calcium and high in lead which suggests that the glass is 18th century or later. There is only a very small trace of selenium and no copper which means that (by a process of elimination) the colorant must be gold. Gold need only be present in 50 parts per million to make red and this would not have been detectable by the techniques used.

Red translucent glass does not seem to have been made in antiquity and gold ruby glass was probably only produced commercially from the 17th century (see W.A. Weyl, *Coloured Glasses* (1951) p.380ff.). The Lycurgus cup which turns to translucent red in transmitted light, however, does contain gold and silver particles but it is dichroic (see D.B. Harden, *Glass of the Caesars* (BM 1987) pp.245-9; D.J. Barber & I.C. Freestone, 'An Investigation of the origin of the colour of the Lycurgus Cup by Analytical Transmission Electron Microscopy', *Archaeometry* 32 (1990) p.33ff.)

Maenad busts of this type belonged to the Neo-Attic tradition and were popular from the 3rd to the 1st century BC (see Plantzos, *Hellenistic*, pp.86-7). They are well-known and there are many different versions of these very finely engraved gems. They have been published many times and a number of copies with slight variations survive. The most famous ancient example is the flat cornelian gem in Berlin where an ecstatic maenad flings her head far back; this is dated ca.70-60 BC (*Berlin*, no.382 (refs.) = *AG*, pl.41.22; *Würzburg*, no.254; Plantzos, *Hellenistic*, no.408). An ancient glass paste from Herculaneum shows a similar maenad with her head only slightly thrown back (*Naples* i, no.55 - glass paste (31.7 x 25mm)).

This gold ruby glass gem and the examples listed below seem to be derived from a less ecstatic maenad type of the 1st century BC, illustrated by the famous and rather larger gem once belonging to Lorenzo dei Medici where the maenad, looking straight ahead, appears rather more sober:

Würzburg, no.253 (= *AG*, pl.41.21; Plantzos, *Hellenistic*, no.412) - a glass paste copy of the original sapphire or amethyst dated second quarter of the 1stc.BC, once in the collection of Lorenzo dei Medici (27.8 x 20.7mm, slightly convex)

The two maenads listed below are very close in detail to the gold ruby glass gem; they also face to the left in impression and are both about the same size (though are smaller than the Medici gem). Both gems, however, are convex rather than flat:

AG, pl.41.23 (= Plantzos, *Hellenistic*, no.413) - a convex cornelian (15 x 12mm) in Paris.

London, no.2950 (= Plantzos, *Hellenistic*, no.417) - a convex 'Greco-Roman' amethyst glass gem (16 x 12mm). An XRF and Raman Microprobe analysis (Project no.7165) carried out by L. Joyner of the Dept. of Scientific Research in the British Museum found that this glass gem has a high lead content and is likely to be a potash-lead-silica glass which shows that it is relatively modern.

Three maenads very close to the type on this gem and the two examples above are published with their plaster casts in Raspe/Tassie 1, nos.4992-4, p.304. No.4993 appears the closest to the gold ruby glass gem but it is a little larger (16.5 x 13.5mm) and slightly convex; it is possibly a cast of *London*, no.2950, or the Paris gem *AG*, pl.41.23. (No.4994 is also quite close; no.4992 is flatter and smaller but the head appears slightly different.)

Wright Gems

21
A winged **Nike/Victory** with a palm branch over her left shoulder and holding out a large wreath in her right hand moves in profile to the right; she approaches a large bird from behind, probably an eagle - but only its tail feathers and part of its body are visible; the Victory wears a *chiton* with overfold and her skirt blows out behind her.

Cornelian ringstone, dark reddish-brown.
13 x 11 x 4mm. (at widest part).   Shape F.1 irregular (the stone has been cut down)
Acquired in Trabzon/Trebizond (Trapezus) on the southern coast of the Black Sea, Turkey   (1942)
Late 2nd century AD Roman Imperial

21   4 : 1

This rather coarsely engraved gem belongs to Kleibrink's 'Imperial Small Grooves style' dated 1st - 2nd century AD (*Hague*, pp.251-2). The body is rather lumpy and details are indicated by small grooves with longer parallel grooves for drapery, feathers etc. which give a patterned effect. A victory engraved on a flat cornelian in the same style is dated to the 2nd century AD (*Vienna* ii, no.1198).

This ringstone has been cut down and half the bird is missing but what must have been the same motif appears on:
Berlin, no.520 - 2ndc.AD convex cornelian; on the left a Victory in similar style, holding out a
    wreath flies towards a large eagle which stands on a low pedestal with its head turned back.
Munich iii, no.2885 - 2nd-3rdc.AD convex cornelian; a vertical arrangement of the same motif.

22

Fortuna-Ceres stands frontally with her head in profile to the left; she wears a *modius* and her hair is arranged in a roll round her head; her weight is on her right leg and her slightly bent left leg can be seen beneath her long, high-girded *chiton*; a *himation* is wrapped round her hips and falls in a fold over her left arm; in her right hand she holds a rudder, a corn ear and poppy capsule and has a cornucopia on her left. Ground line.

Cornelian ringstone, reddish-orange; fine condition.
9 x 7 x 4mm. Shape A.1
Acquired near Sadak (Satala) eastern Turkey (June 1942)
End of the 1st - 2nd century AD Roman Imperial

22   4 : 1

This belongs to the group of small oval, convex gems which Kleibrink includes in the 'Imperial Classicising style' (*Hague*, pp.195-7; and see also **13**) but the engraving of the drapery relates this cornelian gem also to the 'Stripy' and slightly later styles.

This pantheistic goddess holds the cornucopia and rudder, the usual attributes of Fortuna, as well as the corn and poppy head which are the symbols of Ceres. This syncretism appears on gems of the late 1st century AD and continues into the 3rd century AD (see remarks for *Dalmatian Gems*, no.120). Fortuna-Ceres was a very popular motif and appears with various combinations of attributes on numerous gems of different shapes and sizes (cf. **23** here).

For similar types of Fortuna-Ceres with the same attributes, see:
Erimtan, no.85 - light sard (shape A.1) in fragmentary iron ring, 2ndc.AD.
  no.86 - light sard (shape F.2); as above but without a poppy capsule.
Vienna ii, nos.1545-52 - dated 2nd and 3rdc.AD; esp. no.1550 - 2nd-3rdc.AD cornelian with convex
    face and back.
Dalmatian Gems, no.120 - Evans sealing of a gem from Epidaurum; refs.
Lewis, no.105 - convex plasma dated 1st or 2ndc.AD.
Sa'd, no.102ff., esp.no.104 - 2ndc.AD convex cornelian.
Hague, no.836 - 1st-2ndc.AD cornelian engraved in the 'Round head style'.
Aquileia, nos.602-8, pp.240-41.
Naples i, nos.76-7 - a flat sardonyx and a cornelian from Pompeii.
Bologna, no.182 - 2ndc.AD convex cornelian; similar but larger.

23
Concordia-Ceres sits on a stool facing in profile to the right with her body turned in three quarter view to the front; she appears to wear a diadem and her hair is arranged in a roll round her head; she wears a high-girded *chiton* and has a *himation* draped over her legs; on her right she has a cornucopia and in her left hand holds out a *patera* over a large ant with a grain of corn in its jaws. Ground line.

Plasma ringstone with some dark inclusions; fine condition.
10 x 7.5 x 4mm. Shape A.1
Acquired in Antakya (Antioch/Antiochia) in Syria (March 1944)
1st-2nd century AD Roman Imperial

23 4 : 1

This gem resembles some of the intagli in Kleibrink's 'Imperial Small grooves style' of the 1st-2nd century AD (*Hague*, pp.251-2; and cf. nos.682, 684 - seated figures on convex plasmas; also *Erimtan*, no.87 - see below). For small plasma gems see also **36**.

Seated Concordia, holding a cornucopia and *patera*, like the figure on this gem is common on coins from all over the empire from the mid 1st century AD: *LIMC* v, 'Homonoia/Concordia', no.13ff.; *RPC* 2, no.1911 - an aureus of Vespasian AD 70, minted in Syria (Judaea?) with the legend 'CONCORDIA AVG'. (Concordia is also found on coins of Bithynia and Pontus dating to the reign of Vespasian: *RPC* 2, nos.601, 611, 619). Concordia occasionally holds the *patera* out over an altar (*LIMC* v, loc.cit. no.15). This usual type of seated Concordia (sometimes with the altar) appears also on gems: see *Nuremberg*, no.124 - 2ndc.AD convex red jasper (with altar), refs.; *Vienna* ii, no.1570 - 2ndc.AD convex plasma (no altar; discussion and refs. to the type on coins); *F.Berlin*, no.2431 - convex plasma ('Demeter').

On the other hand, the usual type of *seated Ceres* with an ant in the field is shown without a cornucopia and holding corn stalks: see *LIMC* iv, 'Demeter/Ceres' nos.90-91 (= *Vienna* ii, no.1492 and *N.Y.*, no.346). Similarly standing Ceres (as 'Fides Publica'), holding out a plate of fruit is also usually shown with an ant in the field - but one example has an altar instead of the ant: see *LIMC* iv, loc.cit., no.117 (= *Munich* iii, no.2505).

The pantheistic goddess on this unusual intaglio is therefore a conflation of Concordia and Ceres. She is based on the seated figure of Concordia described above but the ant (which takes the place of the altar) links her to the similar seated figure of Ceres who is often shown with an ant in the field. (For the ant with corn in its jaws see *Dreikönigenschreines*, no.280 - a 2ndc.AD red jasper, and as a symbol of fertility and riches, Delatte/Derchain, p.287ff.)

Although there are a number of variations on the seated Ceres type, the Concordia/Ceres combination here has no exact parallel to my knowledge. For other unusual types, compare:
Sa'd, no.121 - 2ndc.AD flat cornelian; conflation of seated Tyche and Demeter; the goddess holds a cornucopia, steering oar and rudder but also holds a corn-ear.
   no.195 - 1stc.AD convex cornelian (shape B.5); seated Demeter/Ceres has a cornucopia and holds corn-ears.
Erimtan, no.87 - a small convex plasma with white surface (shape A.1); same type as *Sa'd*, no.121 (see above) and very close in style to the Wright gem from Antioch.

24

Two Tychai/Fortunae (or Concordiae) stand symmetrically, their bodies in frontal view; they join their right and left hands respectively and each holds a cornucopia on the outside arm; their heads are in profile and both have their hair arranged in a roll round their head and wear a *modius*; the figure on the right wears a high-girded *chiton* and a *himation* wrapped round her hips with the end hanging over her arm; the figure on the left wears a *peplos* with overfold and, although she has no *himation*, she also has a panel of drapery over her arm; they stand in the same way with the weight on one leg and the other one showing through the drapery. Ground line.

Yellow jasper ringstone; in very fine condition
13 x 11 x 3mm. Shape F.1
Acquired in Split, Dalmatia (March 1947)
2nd century AD Roman Imperial

24   4 : 1

This gem is related to Kleibrink's 'Imperial Chin-mouth-nose style' which is dated 1st-3rd century AD (*Hague*, p.294) and is a very fine example of the patterned style which is found especially on jasper gems of the 2nd and 3rd centuries AD. The panel of drapery hanging down beside the figure on the left wearing the *peplos* corresponds to the end of the *himation* on the other figure and was perhaps added for the sake of symmetry.

There are a number of intagli with two Tychai or Fortunae joining (rather than shaking) hands in similar fashion to those on the yellow jasper from Split. They are, however, all engraved in a very different, more cursory style and appear to be dressed identically apart from *Vienna* ii, no.1214, where the Fortuna on the right has a *himation* draped round her hips (as on the jasper gem from Split). The following examples have symbols in the field sometimes relating them to the sun and moon, and three have inscriptions, see:

Sa'd, no.119 - 1st-2ndc.AD flat bloodstone; two Tychai wearing a *modius* or *kalathos* on their heads and each holding a cornucopia extend their free arms to hold hands; in the field above are busts of Helios and Selene; below is the inscription XAPA = 'delight' or 'joy'; and clasped hands of Concordia.

(see also *F.Berlin*, no.8667, *Kassel*, no.82 with same inscription; *Vienna*, no.1214, *Brunswick*, no.113, and *Hague*, no.883 for variants.)

25

A **Figure** (or **Tyche**?) of uncertain identity stands frontally with head in profile to the left wearing a (plumed?) helmet or head-dress with a tie at the back and a *himation* draped round the hips; the figure holds an upright sceptre on the left and has the right arm outstretched; the right leg is straight and rests against rocks; the left leg, seen in profile, is flexed as the figure steps onto a small prow. Ground line.

Cornelian ringstone, dark orange; a few small scratches on the face; set in a modern narrow gold band with a loop for suspension.
ca.15 x 12 x 5.5mm.   Shape A.1.
Unknown provenance
Late 2nd-3rd century AD Roman Imperial

25   4 : 1

This gem is cursorily engraved in Kleibrink's 'Imperial Incoherent Grooves style' dated from the end of the 2nd to the 3rd century AD (*Hague*, p.326; and compare Mars, no.982 - a convex cornelian engraved in similar fashion). The modelling is done with short rounded wheel grooves and there is little detailing.

It is uncertain whether the two lines across the chest indicate the top of a tightly fitting garment or a male torso, but the figure on the intaglio perhaps looks more female than male. It is also unclear whether the figure wears a helmet, a head-dress or just has an elaborate hairstyle. Perhaps a helmet is intended (cf. the helmets with plumes worn by the Tychai on the 4th century AD statuettes: K.J. Shelton, *The Esquiline Treasure* (1981) pls. 36-37).

From the end of the 1st century AD similar figures appear on the coinage of the ports of Amastris in Paphlagonia on the south coast of the Black Sea, Nicomedia in Bithynia on the Sea of Marmora and elsewhere. The figure on the intaglio corresponds closely to the figures on these coin-types except that they wear a simple diadem and hold the spear or sceptre transversely, rather than upright.
   While the figures on the coins closely resemble each other, they show small variations and some look more male than female - compare for example the figures on coins of Domitian (r. AD 81-96) minted in Nicomedia: *RPC* 2, p.105, no.662/1 (=*RecGén*, pl.89,22 (no.35) - 'male figure') where 'the identity of the figure is unsure' and no.662/3 where the figure looks female.
   These figures of uncertain identity have sometimes been thought to represent the Tychai of the cities of Amastris, Nicomedia etc. (but the coins with this figure-type do not appear under *LIMC* vi, 'Nikomedeia' or *LIMC* viii, 'Amastris'). A number of other suggestions have been made:

F. Imhoof-Blumer thought they represented seafaring heroes - perhaps Argos III or one of the argonauts (*Nomisma* 5 (1910) 'Beiträge zur Erklärung griechischer Münztypen', pp.27-9, pl.2, nos.8-9, 11-14 - various types). Recently P. Weiss (*LIMC* ii, 'Astakos' p.902) has supported the suggestion put forward by C. Bosch (*Die kleinasiatischen Münzen der römischen Kaiserzeit* 2, i (Stuttgart: 1935) pp.208-13) that the figures on the coins of Nicomedia might represent the personification of the city of Astakos or the eponymos hero. The inhabitants of the destroyed city of Astakos were re-settled in Nicomedia by Nicomedes I in the 3rd century BC.

Coin types dating from the 1st to the early 3rd centuries AD minted in Nicomedia, but not those minted in Amastris or elsewhere, are listed under *LIMC* ii, 'Astakos', p.902, no.1. The list includes figures in the past identified as 'Tyche of Nicomedia (?)' in *RecGén*, nos.35 (see above), 152, 230, 252, 319; or as 'seafaring heroes' in Imhoof-Blumer, op.cit., pp.28-9, pl.2, nos.11-14.

The closest parallel for the figure on the intaglio appears on a coin minted in Amastris (see **25x**): Imhoof-Blumer, op.cit. pl.2.8 (= **25x**) p.27 - late 2ndc.AD coin of Faustina the Younger, wife of
Marcus Aurelius; on the reverse a 'youthful figure with female hairstyle, naked torso...' with the legend 'AMACTP IANΩN' (= *RecGén*, pl.20,23 (no.116)); see also *BMC Pontus*, pl.20,11 (no.30) - ...'(the city of Amastris?)'.

25x 2 : 1 1 : 1

Late 2nd century AD coin of Faustina II, minted in Amastris (Vienna inv. no. 15337)

26

Herakles/Hercules and **Geryon/Geryones**: the Tenth Labour of Herakles. Herakles with his body in three quarter view and head in profile, steps forward to attack the three-bodied monster, Geryon. The naked hero has his lion-skin over his arm and his club raised in his *left* hand (or his *right* hand when viewed from the impression); the monster has three heads, six legs and appears to hold shields and swords. In the exergue are three roughly engraved letters in positive: E A V (?)

Yellow jasper ringstone
14 x 12 x 3.5mm. Shape F.1
Acquired in Istanbul (Byzantium, Constantinople), Turkey (given by Guy Thompson 1942)
2nd-3rd century AD Roman Imperial

26   4 : 1

This gem is engraved with short rounded wheel grooves and blobs. Features are not clearly marked but Herakles' anatomy has been quite carefully engraved in some detail. The style is similar to several examples in Kleibrink's 'Imperial Incoherent Grooves style' of the 3rd century AD (*Hague*, p.326 and cf. for example no.987). Magical amulets are often engraved in this style (*Hague*, p.350).

The subject, material and the three letters (not retrograde) on this intaglio suggest that it was probably intended as a magic amulet and not as a seal. It would have been used primarily as a charm to ward off the evil eye and protect the owner from harm. On amulets the motif was viewed from the stone itself rather than from the impression and so Herakles approaches Geryon on this gem from the left - i.e. from the same direction as he usually appears on other objects. However, there does seem to be some confusion: on the stone he raises his club in his left hand which is unusual and on the impression it appears correctly in his right hand.

The magical use of Herakles as the averter of evil was attested in antiquity but on magic gems he is usually shown wrestling with the Nemean lion - a motif on gems which was recommended for the relief of colic (Bonner, *SMA*, pp.62-4; *Vienna* iii, nos.2212-4 - red jaspers; *Hague*, no.1115 - a yellow jasper from Asia Minor; Delatte/Derchain, pp.202-06). Perhaps the motif on this gem had a similar purpose. The three letters EAV appear to be meaningless but it may be significant that the same three letters are found at the beginning of an inscription on a magical gem with Herakles and the Nemean lion (ΞEαυο λαβων - Delatte/Derchain, no.278). On another magical gem, again with Herakles and the lion on the obverse, there is a triple Hekate on the reverse and there may be some connection with the triple-bodied Geryon on this gem (see Delatte/Derchain, no.280).

Herakles was popular in the Black Sea area where his cult may have replaced that of a similar local god (*RecGén*, p.102). Herakles and his labours appear often on the coinage of Heraclea (Pontica) modern Benderegli in Bithynia where he was the patron of the town. In the Imperial period Heraklean types predominate and under Septimus Severus, Geta and Gordian (from the late 2nd to early 3rd century AD) a series of medals were struck in Heraclea illustrating most of the Twelve Labours - but not it seems Herakles and Geryon. The Tenth Labour, however, is illustrated on an early 3rd century AD coin of Macrinus from Heraclea - but this shows Herakles with his club raised driving before him the cattle of Geryon (*RecGén,* pl.60.18 (no.173, p.371)).

The scene of Herakles and Geryon appears frequently on Classical sarcophagi and other objects but is unusual on gems (although Geryon appears alone on a number of Etruscan scarabs, *LIMC* iv, 'Geryoneus', no.6a-d). Illustrations of the scene take various forms and there are a number of iconographic types.

The version shown on this intaglio, where Herakles is almost the same size as the 3-bodied and 6-legged monster, is close to the type found on coins of Postumus, AD 267-8 (*LIMC* v, 'Herakles', no.1761 (= no.2516, p.78 with refs.); R. Brauer, 'Die Heraklestaten auf antiken Münzen' in *Zeitschrift für Numismatik* 28 (Berlin:1910) p.79 pl.4, no.7) - except that on the coins Herakles swings his club behind him. However, on a 3rd century AD mosaic floor from Liria in the Madrid Archaeological Museum (where all Twelve Labours of Herakles are illustrated) he holds his club up in front of him as on this gem (*LIMC* v, 'Herakles', no.1741 (= no.2520, p.79)).

27
Theseus and the Minotaur: Theseus stands in profile facing to the right and the Minotaur kneels on one leg in front of him with his torso and head turned to the front and his left arm raised. Theseus restrains the Minotaur by placing his right hand on the Minotaur's shoulder and his left knee on his back; he pierces the top of the Minotaur's head with a small spear or arrow. Ground line.

Jasper(?), brownish-grey intaglio; (small traces of iron and manganese; tested by XRF); the stone, broken into five pieces, is mended but has two large pieces missing from the top and the bottom.
50+(orig.ca.60) x 40 x 4mm. Shape A.3 (slightly convex face, flat back)
Acquired in Istanbul (Byzantium, Constantinople), Turkey (given by Guy Thompson 1942)
Ca.3rd-4th century AD or later?

27   4 : 1

1 : 1

III Roman Republican & Imperial

27   4 : 1

This unusual intaglio is difficult to place and some doubts have been expressed as to its antiquity. However, some pieces of the stone have weathered more than others which suggests they may have been lying apart from each other, and in varying conditions underground. The intaglio's use is uncertain: it is obviously too big for a ringstone but could have been used as a magic amulet or have had some decorative purpose. Amulets are sometimes this size and shape and do not always have an inscription - cf. Bonner, *SMA*, no.218 - bluish-grey limestone (40 x 34 x 6mm; Shape A.3) with a frontal figure of Harpocrates of Pelusium standing in a classical pose; his head, seen in profile, appears engraved in a rather similar style to Theseus'.

If this intaglio is a magic amulet it would be dated ca.1st-3rd century AD (see *Hague*, p.350). Some care has been taken to show anatomical details, but the elongated figures are ill-proportioned, stiff and wooden. The hands and feet of Theseus and the Minotaur are shown as blobs without any detailing.

Theseus pierces the Minotaur's head with a small arrow held in his *right* hand when viewed from the stone which suggests this is the correct view (magic amulets were not used for sealing and so were to be viewed from the stone rather than impression - cf. Herakles and his club and remarks for **26**). On the other hand Theseus is usually placed on the left and the Minotaur on the right of the scene (as they appear on the impression here) but there are a few exceptions (e.g. *LIMC* vi, 'Minotauros', no.63 - a 2ndc.AD Attic coin). This scene does not, to my knowledge, appear on magic amulets; but it might well have done so. Heroes (especially Herakles) as averters of evil were often shown fighting monsters; and it would have been thought that a scene such as this might have had a powerful apotropaic effect (cf. **26**).

The story of Theseus and the Minotaur was very popular with the Greeks and the Etruscans, but less so with the Romans. The scene shown here has a long history and its iconography takes several basic forms (*LIMC* vi, 'Minotauros', p.574ff). In Greek art Theseus' weapon is usually a sword while in Roman art it is most often a club; the small arrow-like weapon used here seems unusual. The two figures look unusually wooden and static and there is no sign of a struggle; their poses are perhaps inspired by the scene on early Greek vases (e.g. *LIMC* vi, 'Minotauros', no.10 – a black figure vase of 550-540 BC shows the Minotaur in the 'kneeling' position). Otherwise the figure of Theseus placing his knee delicately on the Minotaur's back looks as if it might have been adapted from the usual profile type of standing hero with his weight on one leg and one foot raised off the ground (cf. the Theseus inspecting his father's sword on a 1st-2ndc.AD intaglio in *LIMC* vii, 'Theseus', no.10 (= Richter 2, no.322)). The Minotaur had appeared alone in this 'kneeling' or 'running' position on Cretan coins from Knossos (e.g. *LIMC* vi, 'Minotauros', no.4 - 425-400 BC). The Minotaur - whose head is seen from the front on this intaglio in the Etruscan tradition - doesn't pull away from Theseus in the usual fashion but just meekly raises a hand in protest.

The scene appears on coins of the Imperial era but is shown in more lively fashion:
Sylloge Numorrum Graecorum Deutchland, Sammlung von Aulock (Berlin: 1957) pl.24.784 - coin of Severus Alexander (AD 222-235) from Nicomedia which shows the Minotaur on both knees and his arm raised in protest.
LIMC vi, 'Minotauros', no.64 - Attic coin of the late 1st or 2nd century AD; here the Minotaur puts up a struggle and Theseus wields a *pedum* but he places his knee on the Minotaur's back as on the intaglio.

The group also appears on a few engraved gems but is treated differently:
LIMC vii, 'Theseus/These', no.32 - 5th-4thc.BC glass paste scarab.
   no.33 - brown glass paste ca.200 BC; Theseus holds both horns of the kneeling Minotaur who raises his arm to restrain him.
Hanover, no.951 (= *LIMC* vi, 'Minotauros', no.61) - end of 1stc.BC - early 1stc.AD glass paste.

28

An **Eagle stands on a low altar** with its head turned back towards the right and with a wreath in its beak; a palm branch in front of it on the left.

Cornelian ringstone, dark reddish-brown; two chips on the lower left edge
15 x 11.5 x 4.5mm. Shape A.1
Acquired in Trabzon/Trebizond (Trapezus) on the southern coast of the Black Sea, Turkey (1942)
1st century AD Roman Imperial

 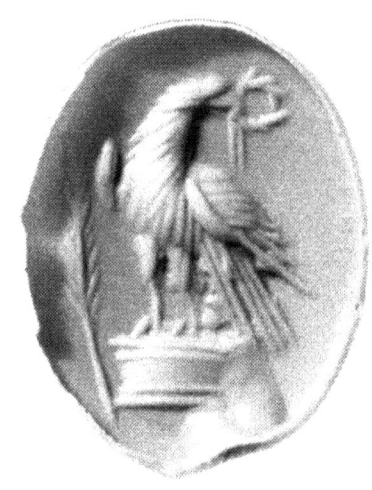

28 4 : 1

A number of eagles on gems are engraved in this style with parallel rounded wheel grooves giving this pleasing patterned effect. The style is related to the 1st century AD 'Imperial Classicising style' (cf. especially *Cambridge*, no.386; *Hague*, no.567).

Eagles with various symbols were popular motifs for soldiers to have on their rings (see remarks for **6** and **7**) and examples have been found all over the Empire - even as far afield as Northern India (Callieri (1997) pl.3, Cat. 1.28 - eagle on an altar with poppy capsule and corn). A number of intagli with eagles also come from Turkey (*Erimtan*, nos.121-7 and see below). The related motif of an eagle, sometimes with a wreath in its mouth, perched on an altar between standards appears frequently on Imperial coins minted in Paphlagonia and Bithynia on the southern coast of the Black Sea.

This is a variant of the more usual type where the eagle has a palm in its beak. However, an eagle (not on an altar) with a wreath in its beak and standing on a palm leaf does appear on coins of Domitian in ca.A.D.95 (*BMC Empire* ii, pl.81,5).

For examples of this variant on gems see:
Erimtan, no.122 - 1st or 2ndc.AD brown nicolo (F.4) back slightly convex; an exact parallel though rather more cursorily engraved.
   no.121 - convex red jasper in fragmentary ring; very close in engraving style and quality but without the palm.
Gaul, no.729 - end of 1stc.BC - 1stc.AD flat white stone (crazed); engraved in the same style; but the eagle actually clasps the palm in its claws; excavated at Metz (Moselle).
Romania, nos.556 - red jasper; as above; also no.555 - serpentine.
Dreikönigenschreines, no.273 - 1st-2ndc.AD dark orange slightly convex cornelian; in linear style similar to this.
Aquileia, no.1266 - jasper; two eagles on altars with a palm; nos.1260ff, refs.p.380.
Sa'd, no.338 - 1stc.AD convex cornelian (shape A.1)

29

A Combination (or ***gryllos***) of *hippalectryon* type walks to the right; it is composed of a cock's legs and feet, and the front part of its body is a bald, bearded Silenus' head surmounted by a horse's head and neck with reins; at the rear is a ram's head with the cock's tail feathers appearing above its nose and a cornucopia behind the horse's neck; a corn ear curves up from the groundline on the left and a palm branch on the right; a star and crescent in the field above.

Cornelian ringstone, orange with lighter shading; very slight scratches on surface
15 x 12 x 6mm. Shape A.4
Acquired in Tarsus on the southern coast of Turkey (1944)
1st century AD Roman Imperial

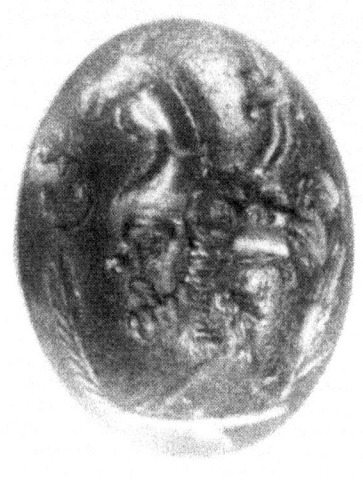 

29 4 : 1

A skilfully engraved gem which compares with Kleibrink's 'Imperial Classicising' and 'Small grooves style' both dating to the 1st century AD (*Hague*, pp.196-8, 251-2).

Grylloi and composite heads (see also **30** and **55**) appear on Greco-Phoenician gems of the 5th century BC and are found also on a collection of seal impressions from a Persian tomb at Ur (see *GGFR*, fig.313, pp.323, 350; *Ionides*, p.35; and A. Roes, 'New Light on the Grylli', *JHS* 55 (1935) pp.232-5 where it is suggested that the Ur sealings are of Persian origin). The later type of *gryllos* came to Rome via Hellenistic Greece and was especially popular between the end of the 1st century BC and the mid 1st century AD. They were probably worn as amulets to avert the evil eye or to ensure the fertility and prosperity of the owner. This example of *hippalectryon* type is very common and Henig dates the type to the 1st century AD rather than earlier (see *Cambridge*, p.129, & no.352). The Silenus heads on these gems have sometimes been compared to heads of Socrates (cf. *Erimtan*, no.98 - 1stc.BC cornelian (F.1)).

There are a number of *grylloi* of *hippalectryon* type very close to this example:
Dalmatian Gems, no.253 - 1stc.AD convex cornelian from Salona (ex coll. Sir Arthur Evans); see
   discussion and references to further examples pp.131-2.
Geneva ii, no.388 - flat jasper (dated 80-40 BC); corn in the ram's mouth; refs.
N.Y., no.545 - convex cornelian; a star and crescent in the field.
Romania, no.587 - reddish cornelian; a star and crescent in the field.
Cologne, no.232 - 1stc.AD dark red-brown cornelian from the Rhineland; a palm branch in the
   field in front and crescent behind.
Erimtan, no.153 - 1stc.AD sard; a variation on the same type with corn and poppy capsule; rather
   more cursory.

30

Conjoined heads: a bald, bearded **Silenus head** is joined to a **ram's head** which appears to have its legs(?) coming out of its mouth.
On the reverse the inscription (not retrograde) in Greek letters:
ΔOMNA KAΛH = 'beautiful woman'

Cornelian ringstone, red; fine condition; in a gold swivel setting.
ca.9 x 7 x 2mm. Shape F.6 or F.8.
Setting: h.20 x diam. of hoop 20mm. The hoop is round in section and the setting which is open behind (to show the inscription) is concave on one side so that it can be worn; ca.1800.
ex Southesk collection (from Phillips, 1878); bought from Spink ca.1950's.
1st century BC Roman Republican

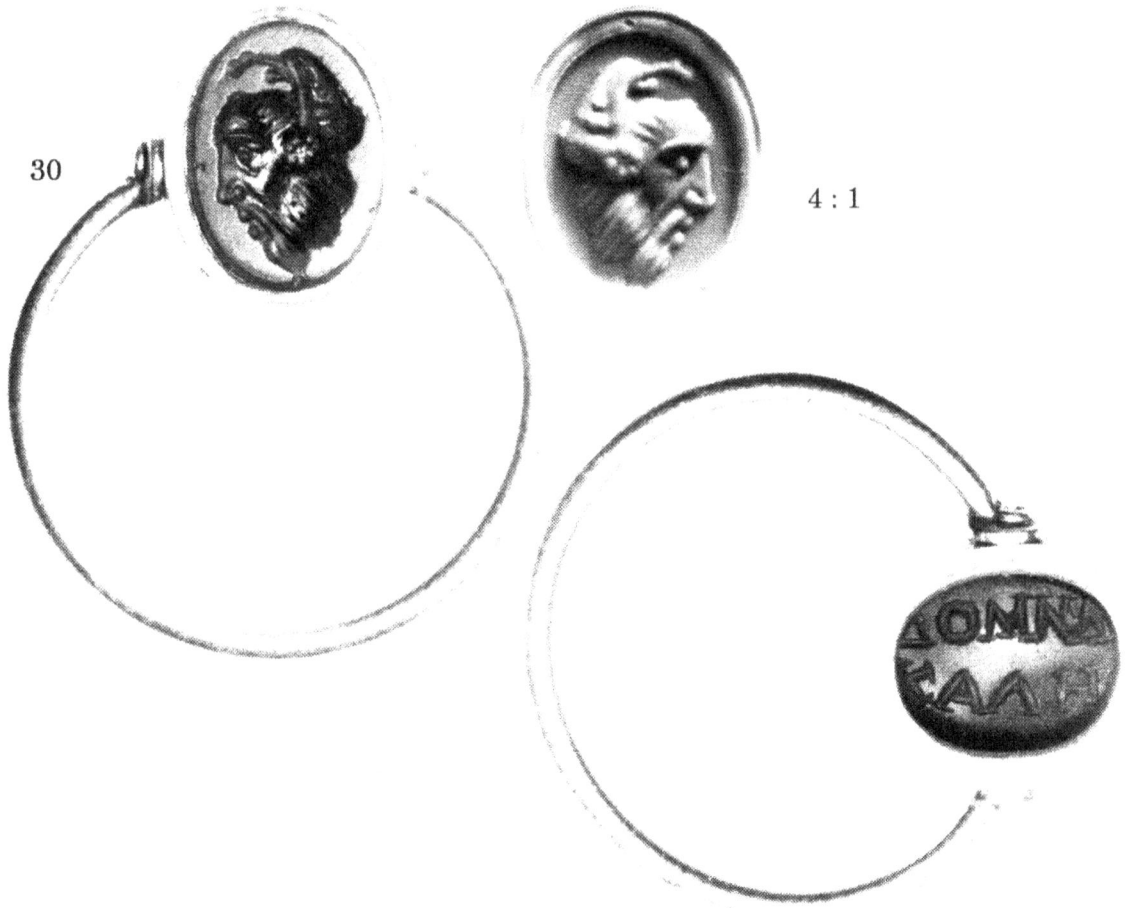

Publ: H. Carnegie, *Catalogue of the Collection of Antique Gems formed by James, Ninth Earl of Southesk* (London: 1908) pl.9, I 7, p.108 ...'An indifferent intaglio on sard. Its sole interest consists in the inscription on the reverse, in honour, no doubt, of the owner's mistress.' (Bought at Phillips, Cockspur St. in 1878)

The remarks in the Southesk catalogue (above) seem unjustified. The gem is of some interest and quite finely engraved. The use of the small round bouterolle drill to mark the features of the Silenus head as well as the horn and eyes of the ram relates the gem to Kleibrink's 'Italic-Republican Pellet style' dated 2nd - 1st century BC (*Hague*, pp.131-2, and compare especially no.189 - a brown glass-paste with ram and goat head combination in similar style). The earlier convex intagli in this group were replaced towards the end of this period by flat stones.

In the Roman period bearded or Silenus heads are combined with a variety of human or animal head or heads (cf. **55**) and often form part of the more complex *grylloi* of *hippalectryon* type (**29**). (The latter sometimes also have the horses' legs sprouting from the Silenus' forehead (e.g. *Munich* i, no.502, Richter 2, no.384)). On the Southesk gem, which is engraved in an earlier style, the arrangement is different and the Silenus' head is 'capped' by the ram's head rather than the horse's head (cf. *Madrid*, nos.381, 383 (below) where the elements are combined in the usual way as they appear on the more complex *hippalectryon* types).

The inscription on the back of the gem is engraved in positive and therefore is to be read from the stone itself rather than from the impression. Similar inscriptions appear on a number of gems, e.g. Richter 2, nos.402-3 (=*LondonRings*, nos.589-90) - ΚΥΡΙΑ ΚΑΛΗ - 'fair lady' and ΑΙΛΙΑ ΚΑΛΗ - 'Ailia is fair'

For related combinations, compare:

GGFR, pl.446, p.287 (= *London*, no.504) - a plasma scaraboid of the early Classical period (ca.480-450 BC); a composite bearded head with ram's head-crest.

Madrid, no.383 - 1st-2ndc.AD flat cornelian; the more usual back to back combination of Silenus and ram's head with corn in its mouth.

  no.381 - 2ndc.AD flat, red jasper; a Silenus head with horse's head on top (and pan's head behind).

Vienna iii, no.2111 - 2ndc.AD convex cornelian; a youthful mask with eagle's head like a Phrygian cap on his head (Ganymede and the eagle); a similar arrangement to the Southesk combination.

31
Medusa mask seen from the front but very slightly turned to the right; the wings on her head and snakes for hair just visible.

Cameo, three-layered agate: white layer/bluish-white layer/and dark layer with some bluish-white chalcedony left on the roughly cut back.
8 x 6 x 5mm
Acquired in Giresun (Cerasus) on the southern coast of the Black Sea, Turkey (December 1941)
ca.3rd century AD

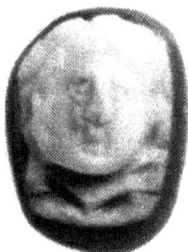

31   4 : 1

This is a rather cursory example of a very common and widespread motif. The Medusa mask functioned as an amulet to ward off the evil eye and protect the wearer. They are difficult to date but Henig has suggested that the better gems are earlier and the more stylised examples like this one are later. A small medusa mask of this type might have been used for setting in an earring. For Medusa masks, see *Content Cameos*, pp.87-92 and also remarks for *Exeter*, no.52, pp.64-5. (For the possible connection, though at a much earlier period, between the profile type of Medusa and Mithradates of Pontus see Plantzos, *Hellenistic,* pp.88-9.)

For frontal Medusa masks, see:
Content Cameos, no.163 - 3rdc.AD; a similar very small, stylised example; refs.
Cambridge, no.535 - 2nd-3rdc.AD same size and quality.
Exeter, no.52 - (chipped) found at Nazareth, Galilee; see list for further examples, some from Asia Minor.
Gaul, no.989 - similar style but larger; from Alésia.

32

Obverse: **Anubis** (or **Seth**?) is shown in Egyptian fashion with his torso seen from the front and his head and legs in strict profile; he wears a short tunic and cuirass(?); he holds a raised sword in his right hand and an *ankh* sign in his left. He has a human body, a dog's (or ass's?) head with a mane and long, pointed ears; a star is in the field on the left and a crescent on the right. Groundline.
Reverse: an inscription reads ΦΙΒΛΟ = Egyptian - 'the ibis' ?

Haematite ringstone
14 x 12 x 5mm.   Shape F.1
Acquired in Tarsus on the southern coast of Turkey (1944)
ca.3rd century AD onwards

32   4 : 1

Magic amulets are thought to have been produced during the later Roman Empire, mostly from about the 3rd century AD onwards - although Pliny (*Nat. Hist.* 23, 41) seems to refer to their being worn in the 1st century AD. The majority come from Syria, Turkey, Egypt and Palestine (see *Hague*, p.350). Haematite was a popular stone for these gems and they are often engraved in a similar style to this example with rounded wheel grooves of various thickness. As these intagli were regarded as charms, rather than seals, the motifs and the inscriptions are to be viewed from the stones themselves rather than the impressions.

The inscription: ΦΙΒΛΟ appears to be a variant of the more usual ΦΙΒΑΟ which forms part of the last word in the Iarbatha formula (Ιαρβαθαγραμνηφιβαωχνηεω). This *logos* or formula was used to invoke the help of the sun in gaining control of a *paredros* or attendant spirit. This formula appears quite often on magic gems and papyri with solar associations (see Bonner, *SMA*, pp.141-2, 205-6; K. Preisandanz, *Papyri Graecae magicae: die griechischen Zauberpapyri* (Leipzig) vol.1 (1973) p.10, line 142). Dr Simone Michel has drawn my attention to W.M. Brashear, 'The Greek Magical Papyri: an Introduction and Survey; Annotated Bibliography' (1928-1994)', *ANRW* 18,5 (1995) p.3587 where various parallels and etymologies for the Iarbatha formula are given. It is suggested that φιβλω (a scribal variant of φιβαο) probably comes from the Egyptian p3-hb = 'the Ibis'. The ibis was the symbol of Thoth and the name of the bird might be applied to the god himself (see R. W. Daniel, *ZPE* 50 (1983) pp.148-9, 152-3). Thoth besides being the magical god of healing, had solar associations (see Delatte/Derchain, pp.141-2). Both the Ibis of Thoth and Anubis sometimes carry the *caduceus* and so were linked to Hermes (Bonner, *SMA*, p.41).

Anubis was one of the principal funerary gods of ancient Egypt. He presided over mummification, took part in funerals and guarded over burials. The Isiac cult of Anubis continued in Egypt during the Greco-Roman period and became particularly popular in Italy and in the Roman provinces. Representations of Anubis are found up until the late 4th century AD. In the Roman period, Anubis, in anthropomorphic form, appears frequently on magic gems in his main roles as *psychopompus* (conveyor of souls) and embalmer, as well as the attendant of Isis. He was also sometimes invoked as protector of the living and must have been thought to have had a powerful apotropaic quality on amulets.

He is shown in various costumes and holding a variety of attributes, but most often he wears a short tunic and holds a caduceus and a palm (e.g. *Kassel*, nos.143-4). Both sword and *ankh* are attributes of Anubis but it is unusual for him to carry both together; he usually carries either one or the other with various other attributes - usually a baton and/or sceptre (see examples below).

On this gem, as a Roman legionary in military dress and with raised sword, he is perhaps shown in his role as guardian of burials and protector of souls against the powers of evil on their voyage to the afterlife. The *ankh*, the symbol of life, probably refers to his role as the procurer of immortality through mummification and guarantor of a new life after death.

Anubis was also thought of as a cosmic deity reigning over the whole world, and as a god of time. Some Anubis gems have a solar theme, and the star (or sun) and crescent moon (symbols of eternity) in the field here may allude to this role (cf. Delatte/Derchain, no.125 - Anubis with crescent and stars; Bonner, *SMA*, no.222ff.). For Anubis see especially Delatte/Derchain, pp.89-103; Bonner, *SMA*, nos.36-44; and on gems and other objects *LIMC* i, 'Anubis', pp.862-73.

On other intagli Anubis is shown with various combinations of attributes; on several he holds an upright sword and on others the *ankh* - but not both attributes on the same gem (although see *LondonMagicGems*, no.381 below):

Hanover, no.1697 - with sword and sceptre.

Hague, no.1128 - dark green jasper; Anubis holding a sword upright in his right hand and with a shield on his left; stars in the field and an inscription; refs.

Delatte/Derchain, no.116 - onyx? Anubis with an *ankh* in his right hand and with a long upright baton on his left.

  no.119 - green jasper; Anubis facing another figure; both with an *ankh* and holding a baton, palm and sceptre.

Campbell Bonner, 'Amulets Chiefly in the British Museum' in *Hesperia* 20 (1951) pp.301-45, no.8 - mottled jasper; Anubis holding an upright sword on his left and in his right hand a serpent (with solar disc).

  no.9 - Anubis holding an *ankh* and sceptres stands before seated Horus; both enclosed by an *Ouroboros*; inscription.

LondonMagicGems, no.381 (= BM no.48954) - 3rd-4thc.AD haematite intaglio with a very similar figure to the one on this gem (though perhaps rather more ass-like) who also holds a sword and *ankh* or *sa* sign.

The identity of this figure (no.381) is uncertain and in the past both Anubis and Seth have been suggested (see *Journal of the Warburg and Courtauld Institutes* 22 (1959), J.G. Griffiths, 'Seth or Anubis?' i, and A.A. Barb, ii, pp.367-371, pl.38a).

During the Imperial period there was some confusion between Anubis and Seth and it is sometimes difficult to distinguish between the two. They often have a very similar appearance; but Seth is supposed to resemble an ass rather than a dog or jackal (see *LIMC* i, 'Anubis', p.872). The inscription on the reverse of this intaglio with its solar connotations (see p. 56) perhaps suggests that the figure on the obverse is more likely to represent Anubis, the cosmic deity linked with the resurrection, rather than Seth, the god of disorder, dark and evil.

33

Draped bust of a beardless youth or **one of the Dioscuri** facing in profile to the right with a star above his head; his hair is arranged in a roll round his head and drapery is gathered at the shoulder and held with a brooch.

Cornelian ringstone, orange
11 x 10 x 4mm. Shape B.3
Acquired in Trabzon/Trebizond (Trapezus) on the southern coast of the Black Sea, Turkey (1942)
2nd-1st century BC Roman Republican

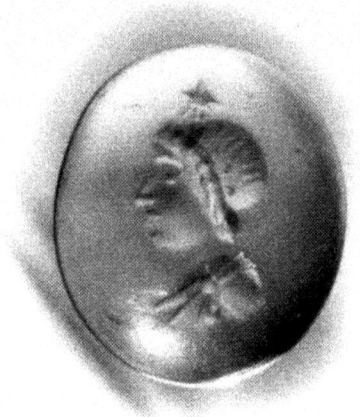 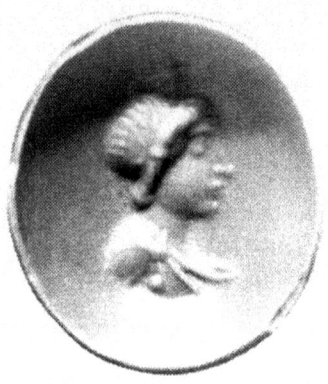

33 4 : 1

The broad oval, convex shape of this cornelian and style of engraving is typical of intagli engraved in the 'Campanian-Roman style' dated from the 3rd to the beginning of the 1st century BC (*Hague*, pp.108-9). Motifs on these intagli are often Hellenistic in origin and the style of engraving can be compared to Campanian coins, terracottas and other objects. Modelling with the large rounded drill and the small round bouterolle pellets used here for the star, hair, eye, nose and mouth etc. are characteristic of this style and also appear on contemporary coinage.

It is uncertain whether this head with a diadem depicts a youthful hero or one of the Dioscuri (Castor or Pollux). The Dioscuri are usually seen together but another single head, 'probably one of the Dioscuri', appears on a cornelian intaglio of the Augustan period engraved in the late Wheel style (*Nijmegen*, no.58).

Portraits of later Ptolemaic kings and princes sometimes have a star over their head as a symbol of apotheosis (cf. the sealings H. Kyrieleis, 'Ptolemäische Porträts auf Siegelabdrücken aus Nea Paphos (Zypern)' in *Archives et Sceaux du Monde Hellénistique...* ed. M-F. Boussac et al, *BCH* Suppl.29 (1996) pl.54ff.).

There are a number of busts in this style, compare:
Hague, no.112 - 2nd-1stc. BC red cornelian; a bust of Hermes/Mercury of very similar type. See refs. for other examples in this style under no.111.
Hanover, no.199 - 1st century BC convex cornelian; female head; similar treatment of hair and features.
Dreikönigenschreines, no.59 - 2nd-1stc.BC Italicising convex intaglio.

34
Bust of beardless man facing in profile to the left; his hair is in fine straight parallel lines; he has a fillet tied round his head with the ties hanging down behind.

Black glass ringstone; (ancient glass; tested by XRF); a chip on the lower face of the stone.
9.5 (diam.) x 3mm. Shape F.1 (with slightly convex face)
Acquired in Rize (Rhizaion, a few miles east of Trebizond/Trapezus) on the southern coast of the Black Sea, Turkey (1942)
3rd-4th century AD Roman Imperial or possibly earlier (?)

 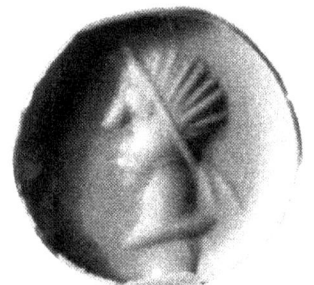

34 4 : 1

A cursory gem, engraved with rounded wheel grooves of various sizes. His eye and nose are roughly drawn with wide wheel grooves and his mouth and chin as two narrower grooves; his hair is shown by fine, straight lines. The engraving style seems related to Kleibrink's late Imperial coarse styles (*Hague*, p.320ff.) dated from the end of the 2nd to the 4th century AD but the gem is difficult to date and it could be rather earlier. Portraits of this type were produced over a long period (cf. the rather finer 1st century BC Republican example, *Berlin*, no.359). Some of these cursory gems may be from provincial workshops (e.g. *Romania*, pls.20-22); and a number of cursory garnet intagli seem to come from a Bosphoran workshop (*Pushkin*, pp.65-6). The head on this glass paste is very similar to the radiate head on a coin of Philip, the Arab, minted in Trapezus, ca. AD 244-5 (*RecGén*, pl.16,10 (p.115, no.54)). Cursory heads comparable to those on provincial gems appear on the coins of the local kings of Bosphorus of the mid 3rd to mid 4th century AD (see *BMC Pontus*, pl.18 especially).

Compare also the following cursory intagli, mostly from the provinces:
Erimtan, no.7 - cornelian (shape F.2) in bronze ring; bust of Apollo but engraved in similar style.
Gaul, no.489 - flat cornelian in 1st - 2ndc.AD ring (type 2c); cursory bust of very similar type with
    long straight neck (Emperor/Julius Caesar?); from Laon.
Romania, nos.419-20, 450, 446, 448 - mostly cornelians.
Kibaltchitch, nos.177, 182 - cornelian gems, a female bust and a mask, from Olbia and
    Panticipaea.
    no.199 - a convex hyacinth.
Hanover, no.1614 - 'Late antique' flat cornelian; bust of man with a fillet round his head and ties
    flying out behind; similar treatment of hair and neck.
Pushkin, no.9 - 1stc.BC-1stc.AD convex almandine with head or mask in an ancient setting.
    no.39 - 1st-2ndc.AD convex almandine in an ancient mount; female head but with similar
    treatment of the neck.
Callieri (1997) pl.1, Cat.1.12 - flat cornelian; head with similar appearance though less cursory
    ('Roman').

Wright Gems

35

Bust of beardless warrior in facing profile to the right wearing a plain helmet with long plume.

Cornelian (or sard) ringstone, darkish brown
10 x 7 x 2.5mm. overall; intaglio face 7 x 5mm. Shape F.2
Acquired in Rize (Rhizaion a few miles east of Trebizond) on the southern coast of the Black Sea, Turkey (June 1942)
3rd-4th century AD ?

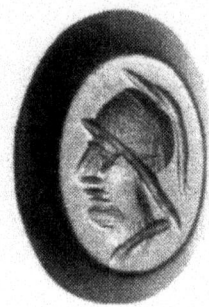
35

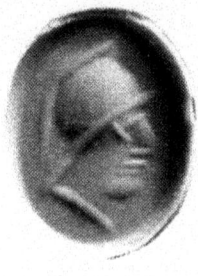
4 : 1

Cursory work rather like **34** but the shape of the gem with bevelled obverse edge relates it more closely to Kleibrink's later Imperial styles (*Hague*, pp.311, 320-21, 326; and compare the head no.867 in 'Chin-mouth-nose-style').

This example, like **34**, can be compared to heads on provincial intagli:
Romania, no.430 - cornelian, helmeted head.
   no.432 - black agate.
   no.436 - three-layered agate.
Pushkin, no.32 - 1st-2ndc.AD convex almandine with head of Athena in a 2nd-3rdc.AD mount.

36

A bearded **Goatherd** with a cap-like hairstyle, wearing a skin cape and short tunic, stands leaning on a staff facing in profile to the right with his left leg bent and right one straight; in front a dog sits looking back at him; on the right of the scene a goat stands on its back legs browsing on the leaves of a tree. Ground line.

Plasma ringstone; some dark inclusions and a small flaw on the face of the stone.
9 x 7 x 4mm. Shape A.1
Bought in Bari, 1942 (?acquired in Zagreb, Croatia; see p.1)
End of the 1st century BC - 1st century AD Roman Imperial

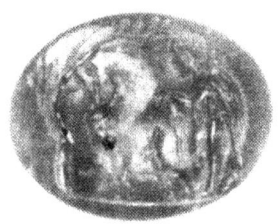 

36 4 : 1

Small convex plasma ringstones like this belong to the Classicising style. They can be dated fairly closely to the 1st century AD, not only because many of the motifs can be attributed to the 1st century AD, but also because stones of this size and shape have been found in 1st century AD ring-types. The style was popular for pastoral scenes, and small figures are often engraved with deep and rounded wheel grooves as they are on this gem (see *Hague*, pp.196-7, and compare no.488 - a small plasma gem in a 1st century AD ring). See also the small plasma gem with seated Ceres (**23**); and also Venus (**13**).

This pastoral scene with slight variations appears on numerous intagli. It was of Hellenistic origin, but in Roman art a version of this motif was sometimes used for Faustulus discovering Romulus and Remus (see comments for *Dalmatian Gems*, no.173, pp.101-2 with refs.).

For scenes very similar to this, see:
F.*Berlin*, no.8279 (= *Tier-und Pflanzen*, pl.15, no.56) - a small Imperial nicolo; exactly the same scene.
Dalmatian Gems, no.173 - sealing from Iader dated end of 1stc.BC-1stc.AD; a slightly more complex scene but engraved in very similar style (refs.).
Hanover, no.978 - a second half of the 1stc.BC convex cornelian with a flat back; exactly the same scene in reverse and with a Victory approaching from behind the tree on the left.
Aquileia, no.772 - 'officina Pastorale', pl.86.4 and refs.
Cambridge, no.208 - an Augustan sard in miniature 'wheel-style' dated second half of the1stc.BC; similar but here there are four goats.
Getty, no.290 - a larger plasma dated to the late 1stc.AD; a variation with suckling kid; from Asia Minor.
Nuremberg, no.250 - 2ndc.AD cornelian; an exact parallel but in more cursory style.

37

Two pigs (a sow in the foreground) stand one behind the other, facing to the right. Ground line.

Cornelian ringstone, yellow; in the remains of an ancient silver ring.
ca.10mm (diam. of stone). Shape (F.1.?); ring bezel ca.12.5 x 5mm.
Setting: the collar holding the stone is scalloped round the edge and the bezel is closed at the back; the hoop is almost entirely missing.
Bought in Bari, 1942 (?acquired in Zagreb, Croatia; see p.1)
1st century BC Roman Republican (Augustan)

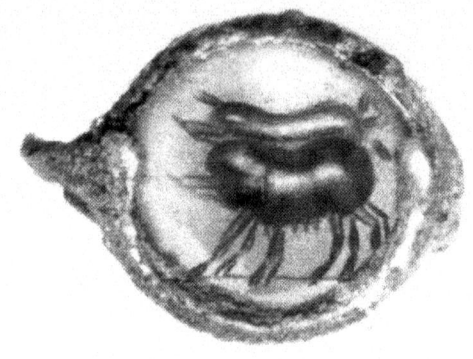 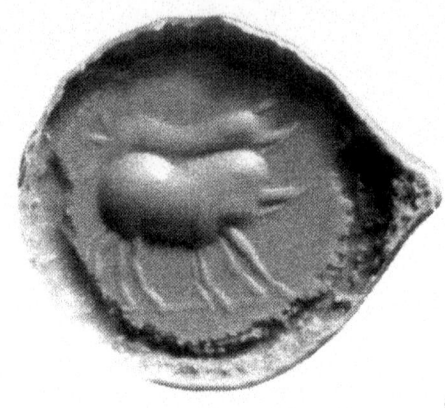

37   4 : 1

There are a number of gems with this motif which are related to Kleibrink's 'Republican Flat Bouterolle style' dated second half of the 1st century BC - AD 30 (*Hague*, pp.179-80, no.426 (below)). The large drill has been used for hollowing out the bodies and details have been added with rounded wheel grooves. The circular shape of the stone is also typical of gems in this style. This seems a popular subject and Sena Chiesa points out that gems of this type (and also **38**) are still related to Italic models (e.g. *Hague*, no.179 engraved in the earlier 'Italic-Republican Blob style' dated ca.200 - first half of the 1st century BC). This intaglio and **38**, another yellow cornelian, are very close in style and motif and show how very similar gems are found in widely separated parts of the Empire.

There are a number of fine 2nd and 1st century BC 'Greco-Roman' examples of this motif; but several in the 'Republican Flat Bouterolle style' are especially close to this intaglio:
Hague, no.426 - 1stc. BC - 1stc.AD cornelian.
Henkel, no.1449 (pls.56, 77 (no.255)) - 1stc.BC-1stc.AD flat cornelian from Mainz; set in an early imperial iron ring; very similar in style to this and the example from Aquileia below.
Aquileia, no.1095 - flat cornelian.
Sofia, no.179 - an almost circular cornelian with flat face; a single pig but engraved in very similar style to this example and **38**.

38
Three pigs: two standing as on **37** and a third mounting the sow in the foreground. Ground line?

Cornelian ringstone, yellow; chipped round the lower, upper and left edges.
ca.11 x 10 x 2mm. Shape F.1
Acquired in Giresun (Cerasus) on the southern coast of the Black Sea, Turkey (December 1941)
1st century BC Roman Republican (Augustan)

 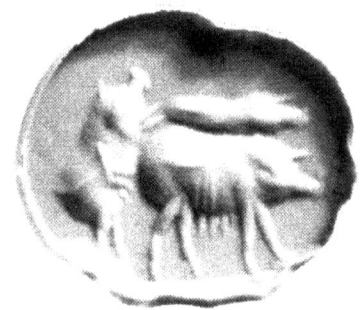

38   4 : 1

See remarks for **37** which is very similar in engraving style and motif. This three-pig motif is also popular and there are examples engraved in various styles - including (as there is for **37**) an earlier intaglio in 'Italic Republican Blob style' of the 2nd-1st century BC (*Hague*, no.180). There are also fine examples in Etruscanising or Hellenising style (*Munich* ii. nos.883-4).

For the same motif in similar 'Flat Bouterolle style', see:
Xanten 2, no.170 - 1stc.AD flat cornelian; similar but more cursory.
Vienna iii, no.1882 - second half of 1stc.AD flat orange cornelian (shape F.1); from Aquileia and probably from a local workshop.
Wellcome, no.36 - Augustan cornelian (shape F.1).

39
Two birds on a fluted fountain. Ground line.

Chalcedony ringstone, opalescent (tested by XRF); gold band round the edge.
ca.8.5 (diam.) x 3.5mm.   Shape F.7
Unknown provenance
1st century AD or modern?

39   4 : 1

This motif is described by Pliny and appears in antiquity on mosaics and other objects (see J. Toynbee, *Animals in Roman Life and Art* (London: 1973), p.259). It was also popular in the 18th and 19th centuries.
Here it is carefully engraved on a very small stone. This example is probably 18th or early 19th century, but one cannot be absolutely certain.

For ancient and modern examples, compare:
Hanover, no.1318 - 1st-2ndc.AD nicolo.
Burton Berry, no.76 - red jasper; quite similar though the fountain is wider and shallower and has handles.
Thorvaldsen, no.1496 – cornelian; two birds pecking at grapes.
Wellcome, no.243 - 19thc. cornelian; two doves drinking from a large stemmed bowl, inscribed 'L'AMITIE'.
Cambridge, no.749 - 18th or 19thc. bloodstone; rather similar to this example; inscribed 'L'AMITIE'.

IV SASANIAN INTAGLI

40
A **lion** springing to the left with its head seen from the front and its ears pricked up; its tail is raised over its back and its claws bared; short parallel grooves indicate its mane.

Cornelian ringstone, brownish-orange
14 (diam.) x 8mm. Shape C.4
Acquired in Trabzon/Trebizond (Trapezus) on the southern coast of the Black Sea, Turkey   (1942)
3rd-4th century AD Sasanian

 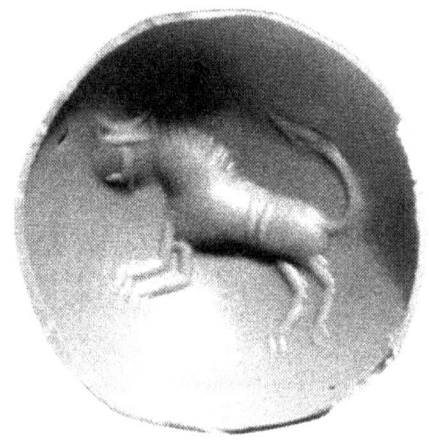

40   4 : 1

This lion is probably Sasanian but its unusual pose and rather cat-like head is not typical. Lions are usually shown sitting, walking or couchant unless they are attacking another animal. However, animals on Sasanian gems do sometimes have their heads outlined in somewhat similar manner. For the lion in Persian iconography see also *N.Y.Sas*, p.94ff.

Compare the following lions:
LondonSass, DD 3 (= Göbl, pl.15, 43a) - 4thc.AD chalcedony ellipsoid.
    DE 5-6 - 7thc.AD cornelian and rock crystal cabouchon; lions with slimmer bodies but heads turned to the front and with quite similar features.
Gignoux & Gyselen, *DCP*, pl.19, no.33,9 - cornelian, decorated ellipsoid; lion leaping on a couchant zebu.
    no.33,10 - chalcedony, similar.

41

A recumbent stag faces in profile to the right with its right leg flexed and its left leg forward.

Cornelian ringstone, cloudy brownish-orange
10 x 9 x 4.5mm. Shape B.3
Ex coll. Prof. A.B. Cook; bought at Sotheby's sale 15/1/1952 (part of lot.89 'Parthian')
Ca. 5th(?) century AD Sasanian

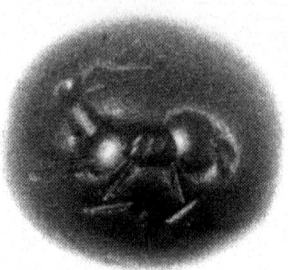 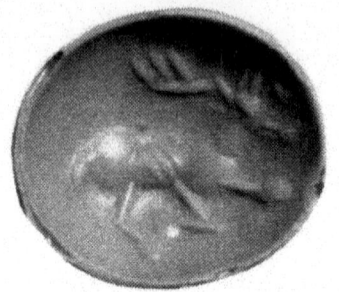

41   4 :1

This stag is quite accurately but simply engraved; a broad drill has been used for the body, and details of ribs, antlers etc. are shown with narrow parallel grooves. A rounded drill has been used for the stag's eye and muzzle.

From prehistoric times stags appeared in Iranian art on all sorts of objects besides seals (e.g. on reliefs and silverware). Stags seem to have had no mythological significance and are shown naturally rather than winged (see *N.Y.Sas*, pp.87-90, and for stags in this position on seals, no.216ff.). It is a common motif on Sasanian seals and is engraved in a variety of styles; several are close to this example.

The following stags seated in the same position are very similar:
LondonSass, FB 4 - 3rd-4thc.AD circular garnet with convex face and flat back.
BN/LouvreSass i, 30.J.17 - flat agate ringstone; stag with one front leg forward.
   30.J.24 - flat agate ringstone; the stag has both front legs tucked under its body.
Gignoux & Gyselen, *BSS*, AMO pl.9, no.30.58 - convex cornelian; an antelope engraved in very
   similar style.

42
A **bird** (a partridge?) with a short tail, round body and with feathers sticking up on its back walks in profile to the right; beading round the edge.

Cornelian ringstone, orange; fine condition, polished
10mm (diam.) x 3.5mm. Shape B.3
Ex coll. Prof. A.B. Cook; bought at Sotheby's sale 15/1/1952 (part of lot.89 'Parthian')
5th century AD Sasanian

42   4 :1

This bird has a shorter tail and is rather more carefully engraved than the ducks (**44** and **45**). Its feathers are shown by short parallel rounded grooves running in different directions.

Several birds are close to this, compare:
LondonSass, HC 2 - 5thc.AD cornelian ringstone with convex face and flat back; a partridge walking to the right, also within a border of dots; a very close parallel; (also HC 1, HC 3-4).
BN/LouvreSass i, 30.S.20 - 30.S.21 - layered agate ringstones; geese (?)

43

A **pheasant** with ear-tufts and recurved tail feathers walks in profile to the left; it has an object (a lizard?) in its beak.

Cornelian ringstone, orange with yellow patches and darker streaks
12mm (diam.) x 6mm. Shape C.3
Ex coll. Prof. A.B. Cook; bought at Sotheby's sale 15/1/1952 (part of lot.89 'Parthian')
ca.6th century AD Sasanian

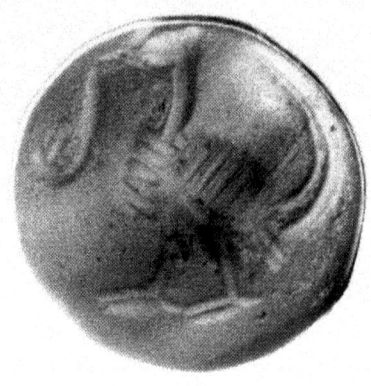 

43 4 :1

There are a number of pheasants on convex Sasanian ringstones engraved with rounded grooves of varying thicknesses in very similar style to this gem. The parallel grooves for feathers give a pleasing patterned effect. Brunner (*N.Y.Sas*, p.109) points out that the pheasant can be shown with straight tail feathers or with them curling up behind to fit neatly into the contour of the stone as they do here.

The pheasant was a popular motif both on Sasanian silverware as well as seals (see Kent & Painter, *Gold and Silver*, p.148, no.312 - a pheasant with recurved tail feathers decorating the roundel of a 4th-5thc.AD silver dish). For the pheasant in Sasanian art, see also *N.Y.Sas*, p.109 and references.

For similar birds, not always identified as pheasants, and without the lizard, see:
LondonSass, HF 6-7 - 6thc.AD cabouchons, a cornelian and a rock crystal; 'bird with upswept tail'.
   HF 8 - 6thc.AD flat garnet; a similar bird pecks at tray of fruit (?)
N.Y.Sas, p.109, no.29 - a sealing (style C) from Qasr-I Abu Nasr (= *QAN*, p.39, pl.iv/11); pheasant with ear-tufts and recurved tail feathers.
Kibaltchitch, no.50 - convex cornelian from the Taman Peninsula; also no.59.
Gignoux & Gyselen, *BSS*, AMO pl.9, no.30.77 - convex cornelian; a very similar bird with recurved tail feathers.
   MCB pl.20, no.30.46 - as above.

44
A **bird** (a duck?) walks in profile to the right.

Cornelian ringstone, orange with yellow patches and darker streaks; fine condition, polished face
10 x 8.5 x 5mm. Shape C.3
Ex coll. Prof. A.B. Cook; bought at Sotheby's sale 15/1/1952 (part of lot.89 'Parthian')
ca.6th century AD Sasanian

 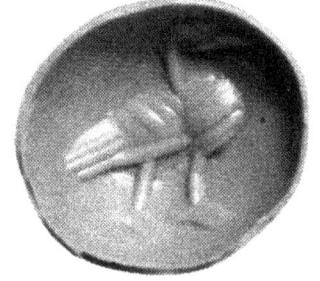

44   4 : 1

This ringstone and the next example (**45**) are engraved in similar style to the pheasant (**43**). Birds are very common on Sasanian seals but many, like this and the next example (**45**), are difficult to identify. There are a number of birds which are close in style to these two but they sometimes have feathers sticking up on their back. The birds on these two gems most resemble ducks which were popular motifs in Sasanian art and also appear on textiles and silver (see *N.Y.Sas*, pp.109-10 for references). They appear related to a group of cornelian or garnet circular gems which have a convex face and concave back (see *Merz*, no.18, p.13).

For very similar birds on ringstones, see:
Merz, no.18 - 6thc.AD convex cornelian with concave back.
BN/LouvreSass i, 30.S.28 - 30.S.36 - convex gems with duck-like birds.
   30.S.31 & 30.S.32 - convex dark green (glass?) gem and garnet in a mount.
Sa'd, no.435 - 5thc.AD flat cornelian (Shape F.4); a duck (?) in very similar style.
Erimtan, no.169 - 5th or 6thc.AD cornelian (Shape C.4)
Callieri (1997) pl. 17, Cat.6.17 – small convex garnet with a very similar bird; probably of local (north-west Indian) origin (Sir J. Marshall coll.).

Wright Gems

45
A **bird** (a duck?) with long beak walks in profile to the to the right.

Cornelian ringstone, opaque with darker streaks and patches of white etching.
10.5 x 9.5 x 5mm. Shape B.3
Ex coll. Prof. A.B. Cook; bought at Sotheby's sale 15/1/1952 (part of lot.89 'Parthian')
ca.6th century AD Sasanian

45   4 : 1

See discussion and examples given for **44**. This bird is very similar but has a longer beak. The ringstone is slightly more oval in shape than the last and there are white patches ('etching') on the body and beak of the bird as well as round the edge of the stone.

46

Two figures (Gemini or the **Dioscuri**?) stand facing each other; the figure on the right has his left hand on his hip and right hand raised holding out a flower(?), and the figure on the left has his hands on his hips; both wear a diadem and have drapery billowing out behind; eight spheres in the field and the sun or a star above. Two short ground lines beneath the figures.

Cornelian ringstone, orange
14.5 x 12 x 2mm. F.4 (flat face, bevelled edges with slightly convex back; very thin)
Acquired in Trabzon/Trebizond (Trapezus) on the southern coast of the Black Sea, Turkey (1942)
ca. 7th century AD Sasanian

46   4 : 1

The engraving style is cursory and difficult to place but the figures do resemble some of the stylised figures or monkeys on Sasanian or 'late Roman' gems (see below). The skirts billowing out behind seem to be derived from drapery on classical figures (cf. Athena's skirt, Delatte/Derchain, no.41, p.212).

It is unclear what the figures represent but the sun and globes in the field seem to suggest an astral context and so perhaps they represent Gemini or the Dioscuri wearing diadems. The figure on the right, however, holds an object (a flower) up to the face of the other figure - a characteristically Persian gesture.

Compare the following pairs or groups of figures:
Kassel, no.152b - reverse of a 4th - 5thc.AD green jasper gnostic gem; two warriors with a spear between them; in rather similar very cursory engraving style.
Kibaltchitch, no.259 - cornelian; two figures wearing helmets and long garments; but in a rather different engraving style; East Greek work ?
Thorvaldsen, no.1747 - cornelian shaped like a truncated cone; two dancing (Bacchic?) figures.
  no.1752 - cornelian; probably two monkeys (rather than Herakles attacking a centaur); on either side a star and a small globe at the top; late Roman - 'very rude work'.
LondonSass, GA 2-4 - pairs of monkeys; GA 4 appears to have stars in the field.
Cambridge, no.911 - 4thc.AD cornelian ringstone (shape F.6); two monkeys with crosses (or stars?) in the field.

Gignoux & Gyselen, *DCP*, pl.5, no.10.45 - figures engraved in somewhat similar manner.
   pl.5, 10.48ff.- stylised figures and animals.
   pl.6, no.11.12
Erimtan, no.76 - sard in ring fragment (shape F.2) 3rdc.AD; a very cursory Nike with similar drapery and figure; legs and feet simple shown as simple grooves and a long groove for her neck.

V LATE ANTIQUE INTAGLI

47
A **Beardless male bust** (Helios/Sol?) facing in profile to the left wearing a head-dress (a Phrygian cap or rayed (?) crown) with hair showing beneath it; heavy drapery over his shoulders.

Dark green stone cameo with lighter flecks (serpentinite or chlorite?)
17 x 10 x 5mm. Pointed oval shape.
From the Black Sea area, Turkey
Late antique? Byzantine?

47 4 : 1

The cutting is rather rough and his head-dress is unclear. He may be wearing a Phrygian cap or if a radiate crown is intended this may depict Helios/Sol (cf. *Munich* iii, no.2210), or perhaps an emperor as Sol (e.g. Kent & Painter, *Gold and Silver*, p.165, no.375 - a gold solidus dated AD 317 with Constantine I wearing a radiate crown).

This green stone cameo is also somewhat reminiscent of an irregularly shaped garnet cameo in a gold pendant setting which was found in Epsom, Surrey, and which is engraved with the bearded head of a man wearing a Phrygian cap. The garnet cameo is also probably from the east and perhaps of similar date to the green stone cameo but the engraving is rather finer. It is suggested that the garnet cameo is late antique and was reset in the 7th century AD (see *Britain*, no.734 = Kent & Painter, *Gold and Silver*, no.295).

48

A winged (bearded?) figure stands facing to the left in profile holding a wreath(?) in his left hand. Alpha and Omega (shown as A and O) in the field on either side of the figure. Ground line.

Steatite ringstone, pale green opaque with dark green patches on the edges.
12.5 x 9 x 4mm overall; intaglio face 9 x 6mm. Shape F.2 (rectangular).
Acquired in Kayseri (Caesarea), Cappadocia, central Turkey (October 1943)
ca.4th century AD onwards - Late Antique or Byzantine Christian?

48   4 : 1

The style of this engraved gem is difficult to place and so its date is uncertain. The body of the figure is covered with shallow vertical grooves - possibly to indicate clothing or feathers. The arm is rather lifeless and engraved as two straight grooves.

The A and O in positive suggest that this is an amulet and so was to be viewed from the stone itself rather than the impression. The substitution of 'O' (omicron) for 'Ω' (omega) is unusual but is attested from the 5th century AD in Syria and elsewhere (*DACL*, vol.1, col.5).

Steatite is quarried in Cappadocia and near Constantinople and it was used for icons in the Byzantine era. It was supposed to have had curative and apotropaic qualities and so was a popular material for amulets. This pale green colour was the most prized (for the material see I. Kalavrezou-Maxeiner, *Byzantine Icons in Steatite*, 2 vols. (Vienna, 1985) pp.70-73).

Winged cupids or putti carrying wreaths appear, of course, on Roman intagli (e.g. *Mira et Magica*, no.21; *Hague*, no.378) but the figure here is perhaps more closely related to the winged (or 'Victory') figures carrying diadems on Sasanian seals which represent the Iranian conception of Royal Glory conferred by victory. As A.D.H. Bivar points out, these figures, unlike those of classical art, are usually male and are sometimes part man and part bird (*LondonSass*, p.27 and no.BK 1ff.; *BN/LouvreSass* i, 40.A.1ff.; *Jerusalem*, P.B.I., no.70, p.163). The engraving style on the Sasanian seals, however, is very different and the diadems have streamers.

A and Ω are found in both Christian and gnostic contexts where the letters had a magical meaning. As the first and last letters of the Greek alphabet, they represented the whole alphabet and thus the entire cosmos. A.D.H. Bivar suggests (personal comment) that the figure might be interpreted in various ways: perhaps it is a pagan cupid with a wedding or engagement ring, symbolising eternal love; or if Christian, an angel bringing the wedding crown of the Greek Church.

Cupids or winged putti are shown carrying wreaths:
Mira et Magica, no.21 - Putto with wreath and a palm.
Hague, no.378 - Cupid with wreath and palm in front of a herm.
Callieri (1997) pl.4, Cat. 2.5ff. – various winged Sasanian male figures carrying crowns or wreaths.
  pl.14, Cat.5.7 & Cat.5.9 – winged Cupids with wreaths and palm; the iconography is Western but the engraving is probably local (north-west Indian).

VI RENAISSANCE & MODERN INTAGLI

49
A **warrior** (**Ares/Mars**?) with a plumed helmet stands frontally with his head turned in profile to the left; he wears a garment with a long V neck and baggy trousers; he holds his spear on his right and rests his shield on the ground on his left. Ground line.

Plasma ringstone
11 x 8 x 2.5mm overall; intaglio face 9.5 x.7mm. Shape F.2
Acquired in Rize (Rhizaion a few miles east of Trebizond) on the southern coast of the Black Sea, Turkey (1942)
Late antique or 17th - 18th century?

49

4 : 1

The gem is engraved with rounded drills of different sizes without much attention to detail. His limbs look rubbery and his hands and feet are shown as simple blobs. Like the figure on **50** he wears a garment with a V-neck. His baggy trousers are Oriental rather than Roman.

50

A **figure holding a flag** in his right hand stands by a wall (or on a ship) with his left arm raised; he wears a garment (perhaps a jerkin or tabard) with a long V-neck, a short pleated tunic and a small cap.

Cornelian ringstone, reddish-brown
12 x 10 x 3mm. Shape F.2 (with slightly convex face)
Acquired in Trabzon/Trebizond (Trapezus) on the southern coast of the Black Sea, Turkey (1942)
16th or 17th century? (Italian?)

50   4 : 1

Engraved in a rather similar style to **49** but he is wearing Renaissance costume.

This figure is somewhat reminiscent of the much earlier standing figures of the emperor on the prow of a galley on the mid 4th century AD coins of Constans (e.g. J.P.C. Kent, *Roman Coins* (1978) no.666 - Maiorina of Constans, AD 349).

VI Renaissance & Modern

51
Athena/Minerva stands frontally with her head in profile to the right; she has a plumed helmet with visor raised and appears to wear a cuirass; she has drapery round her legs; on her right she holds an upright spear and in her left hand she holds a wreath with an unidentifiable object (her shield?) beneath it; on the left of the field an owl perches on an altar. Ground line.

Red lead glass ringstone (tested by XRF)
12.5 x 8.5 x 4mm overall; intaglio face 11 x 7mm.   Shape F.4
Acquired in Sinop (Sinope) on the southern coast of the Black Sea, Turkey (1943)
18th or 19th century lead glass

51   4 : 1

This gem is perhaps moulded rather than engraved. Not all the details are clear and the rather heavy-weight Athena appears to have no feet. The figure is probably copied from an ancient example of the motif where Athena sometimes holds a wreath rather a Victory. The figure of Athena on a gem in Paris seems close in style (see Richter 2, no.102 below).

The following ancient examples are mostly rather different in style, but compare :
Richter 2, no.102 - imperial banded chalcedony; an Athena of similar proportions and style; she
    holds a Nike on her hand; her shield is on the ground beside her and an upright spear behind;
    trees on either side and an owl standing on a pillar beside her.
Aquileia, no.127 - Athena holding a wreath; with an owl, wreath, spear and shield.
Munich iii, no.2474 - beginning of 2ndc.AD flat cornelian; standing Athena of Parthenos type,
    holding a Nike over an owl sitting on the ground in front.

52
Ajax, son of Oileus king of Locris, is seated naked facing to the front on a pile of rocks; his body is turned slightly to the right and his head slightly to the left; his right leg is straight and his left leg is flexed and seen in profile; he wears a close-fitting helmet with small plume; in his right hand he grasps a boulder and on his left holds his large round shield and spear behind.

Amethyst coloured *glass* ringstone (tested by XRF)
17 x 11 x 5mm. Shape A.1 (face very slightly convex and bevelled edge; convex back)
Unknown provenance (bought at Petworth 1953)
18th or 19th century

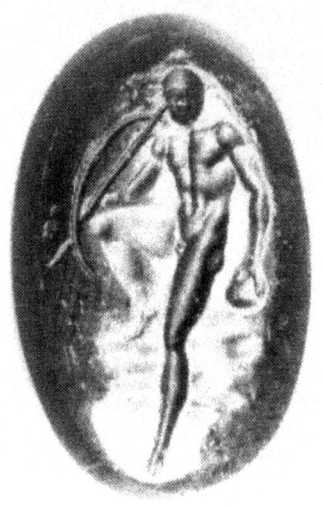 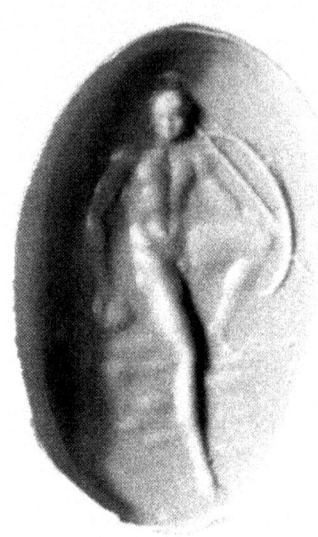

52 4 : 1

This rather elongated figure is sometimes identified as Diomedes and there are a number of copies of the motif with slight variations. An 18th century sard, once in the Blacas collection and which is slightly different to this example is ascribed to Luigi Pichler (*LondonPCG*, pl.29, no.829).

This appears to be a copy of an original convex cornelian of the first half of the 18th century which was once in the Marlborough collection, see:
Raspe/Tassie 2, no.9373, p.547 (and plaster cast).
Würzburg, no.895 - see refs. and further examples.

53

Head or bust of beardless warrior (or **Athena**?) in profile to the right wearing a plumed helmet with visor raised.

Cornelian ringstone, red (tested by XRF); a large chip off the right lower edge and a smaller one on the left.
ca.12.5 x ca.9 x 2.5mm overall. Shape F.1/F.4
Unknown provenance
Probably modern (rather than 1stc.AD)

53 4 : 1

This appears to be a bust of Athena; she has long hair beneath her helmet but her shoulder is chipped off so there is no sign of an *aegis* to identify her. The helmet, however, does not look ancient and the gem is probably modern. The face and head have been engraved with wide, smooth drill grooves and details added with smaller rounded wheel grooves. This head seems rather different to ancient busts of Athena on gems (cf. *Munich* ii, no.2180ff.) but it could be provincial work.

The gem is quite similar to:
Kibaltchitch, no.238 - cornelian acquired in Kertch.
Wellcome, no.222 - Neo-Classical period, later 18th or early 19thc.; Ceres or Proserpina; similar treatment of features.

54

Bust of a bearded warrior wearing a plumed helmet with the visor raised; ties or drapery on his shoulders.

Cornelian (sard) ringstone, dark brown
8 x 6.5 x 3mm. Shape F.1 (with slightly bevelled upper edge)
Acquired in Giresun (Cerasus) on the southern coast of the Black Sea, Turkey (December 1941)
ca.18th or 19th century?

54 4 : 1

This intaglio and the next example (**55**) have a very similar appearance and may have come from the same workshop. Both come from Giresun; they are sards of the same shape and colour, and are engraved in a similar and rather distinctive style. The engraving is careful and precise but it is very shallow; details are added with small rounded drills and fine, straight narrow grooves. This warrior head puts into question the antiquity of the combination head (**55**) which does look more ancient (cf. **55** and see remarks).

The warrior's helmet is unusual and does not look typically ancient. The unattached ties or drapery floating round his neck rather resemble the snakes of Athena's aegis and may have been mistakenly copied from a bust of the goddess.

Compare:
Romania, no.748 - a bearded head engraved in quite similar style to this and **55** but it is dated to the 'Middle Ages'.

55

Conjoined heads or **masks**: a **female head** with fine, straight hair, facing in profile to the right is combined with a bald **Silenus head** turned upside down and facing upwards to the left; the stylised hair/beard separating the two heads resembles a beaded head-band or wreath.

Cornelian (sard) ringstone, dark brown; fine condition.
10 x 7 x 3mm. Shape F.1 (with slightly bevelled upper edge)
Acquired in Giresun (Cerasus) on the southern coast of the Black Sea, Turkey (December 1941)
ca.18th or 19th century?

55   4 : 1

This intaglio is engraved in a similar style to the previous example (see remarks for **54**). The larger areas of the heads are hollowed out with smooth, wide drill grooves and details of features etc. carefully added with small, rounded drills and fine, narrow grooves. A number of other combination heads have similar wispy, straight hair (e.g. *Romania*, no.615) and also the same beaded treatment of the beard/hair (*Munich* iii, no.2225 - see below).

The conjoined heads on this gem look very similar in style to two intagli which are thought to be ancient: the first is from Turkey (also a dark sard of the same size and shape) and the second is from Bulgaria (see examples below). Double head combinations with one head or mask on top of the other, rather than back to back, seem relatively uncommon, but compare the following:

Erimtan, no.151 - flat dark sard (11 x 7mm) in a 1stc.AD gold ring; very similar in style and arrangement to the gem from Giresun; masks of two men with beaded beards and one with wispy hair.
  no.152 - 1stc.AD flat cornelian (shape F.4.); a triple head combination engraved in a very similar style; perhaps from the same workshop as no.151.
Sofia, no.261 - flat cornelian dated 2ndc.AD; the 'shallow carving' is noted in the description and it is almost identical to *Erimtan*, no.151 above.
Munich iii, no.2225 - 1stc.BC convex cornelian; a triple head combination with similarly engraved features and the same stylisation of hair/beard.

Wright Gems

56
Bust of a bearded warrior facing in profile to the right wearing a plumed helmet with visor raised.

Haematite ringstone; fractured and mended.
10 x 6.5 x 4mm overall; intaglio face 9 x 5mm. Shape F.4 (rectangular)
Acquired in Rize (Rhizaion a few miles east of Trebizond) on the southern coast of the Black Sea, Turkey (1942)
ca.19th century.

56

4 : 1

Besides 57, compare:
Nijmegen, no.204 - 'after the antique' 18th-19thc. blackish opaque glass paste; helmeted bust of Mars or Roma.

57

Bust of a bearded warrior facing in profile to the right wearing a plumed helmet with visor raised and a spike on top.

Black glass ringstone; very shiny surface
12 x 8 x 2.5mm overall; intaglio face 10.5 x 6mm. Shape F.2 (upper and lower edges convex and the motif engraved in a concave oval)
Acquired in Aleppo (Bereoa), Syria (January 1943)
19th century

57 4 : 1

For similar gems, compare:
Erimtan, no.171 - 19thc. red opaque glass imitating jasper; also rectangular but without the concave oval (shape F.4)
Jerusalem, p.62, S.B.F., no.55 - orange red cornelian; the stone is the same size and exactly the same shape as the example from Aleppo and the head is in similar style, but this example is dated 1st-2ndc.AD.

Wright Gems

58

Bust of a bearded warrior with plumed helmet and visor raised facing in profile to the right; a spear below.

Glass, cloudy orange-brown ringstone (imitating cornelian)
18 x 13 x 2 mm overall; intaglio face 16.5 x 12mm. Shape F.2
Acquired in Aleppo (Bereoa), Syria (January 1943)
19th or 20th century

58 4 : 1

Compare:
Sa'd, no.469 - modern cornelian; Athena/Roma with a spear in front of her neck.
Bari, nos.138-40 - busts of doubtful antiquity; engraved in a very different style to this gem and **59** but they also have a sword lying diagonally in the field in front.

VI Renaissance & Modern

59
Bust of a bearded warrior wearing a plumed helmet facing in profile to the right; a sword or mace below.

Glass, cloudy pale green ringstone (imitating plasma)
13 x 10 x 2mm overall; intaglio face 12 x 8mm. Shape F.2
Acquired in Aleppo (Bereoa), Syria (January 1943)
19th or 20th century

59   4 : 1

This glass gem is of the same manufacture as **58**

Wright Gems

Abbreviations

(AGDS) Berlin etc. -
Antike Gemmen in deutschen Sammlungen - see Berlin, Brunswick, Hanover, Kassel, Munich, Nuremberg

AG -
A. Furtwängler, *Die Antiken Gemmen* 1-3 (Leipzig, Berlin: 1900)

AGGems -
J. Boardman, *Archaic Greek Gems, Schools and Artists in the Sixth and Early Fifth Centuries BC* (London: 1968)

ANRW -
Aufstieg und Niedergang der Römischen Welt

Ant. Jnl. -
The Antiquaries Journal, being the Journal of the Society of Antiquaries of London

Aquileia -
G. Sena Chiesa, *Gemme del Museo Nazionale di Aquileia* (Padua: 1966)

BABesch -
Bulletin Antieke Beschaving

BAR -
British Archaeological Reports

Bari -
G. Tamma, *Le Gemme del Museo Archeologico di Bari* (Bari: 1991)

BCH -
Bulletin de correspondance hellénique

Berlin -
E. Zwierlein-Diehl, *Antike Gemmen in deutschen Sammlungen 2: Berlin* (Munich: 1969)

BIFAO -
Bulletin de l'Institut Français d'Archéologie Orientale

BMC -
British Museum Catalogue (of Coins)

BMC Empire -
H. Mattingly & R.A.G. Carson, *Coins of the Roman Empire in the British Museum* 1-6 (London: 1923-1964)

BMC Republic -
H.A. Grueber, *Coins of the Roman Republic in the British Museum* (London: 1910)

BN/LouvreSass -
R. Gyselen, *Catalogue des sceaux, camées, et bulles sassanides de la Bibliothèque Nationale et du Musée du Louvre*, i. *Collection Général* (Paris: 1994)

Bologna -
A.R. Mandrioli Bizzari, *La collezione di gemme del Museo Civico archeologico di Bologna* (Bologna: 1987)

Bonner, *SMA* -
C. Bonner, *Studies in Magical Amulets, chiefly Graeco-Egyptian. University of Michigan Studies, Humanistic Series* 49 (Ann Arbor: 1950)

Britain -
M. Henig, *A Corpus of Roman Engraved Gemstones from British Sites, BAR* 8, 2nd ed. (Oxford: 1978)

Brunswick -
V. Scherf, *Antike Gemmen in deutchen Sammlungen* 3: *Braunsweig* (Wiesbaden: 1970)

Burton Berry -
B.Y. Berry, *Ancient Gems from the Collection of Burton Y. Berry* (Indiana: 1968)

Caerleon -
J.D. Zienkiewicz, *The Legionary Fortress Baths at Caerleon. 2 The Finds* (Cardiff: 1986)

Callieri (1997) -
P. Callieri, *Seals and Sealings from the North-West of the Indian Subcontinent and Afghanistan (4th Century BC - 11th Century AD)* (Naples: 1997)

Cambridge -
M. Henig, D. Scarisbrick & M. Whiting, *Classical Gems: Ancient and Modern Intaglios and Cameos in the Fitzwilliam Museum, Cambridge* (CUP: 1994)

Cologne -
A. Krug, *Antike Gemmen im Römisch-Germanischen Museum Köln (1981)* = *Bericht der Römische-Germanischen Kommission* 61 (1980)

Content Cameos -
M. Henig, *The Content Family Collection of Ancient Cameos* (Oxford & Maine: 1990)

DACL -
F. Cabrol & H. Leclerq, *Dictionnaire d'archéologie chrétienne et de liturgie*, 15 vols. (1907-1953)

Dalmatian Gems -
S. E. Hoey Middleton, *Engraved Gems from Dalmatia, from the Collections of Sir John Gardner Wilkinson and Sir Arthur Evans in Harrow School, at Oxford and elsewhere* (OUCA: 1991)

Delatte/Derchain -
A. Delatte & P. Derchain, *Bibliothèque Nationale. Les intailles magiques gréco-Égyptiennes* (Paris: 1964)

Dreikönigenschreines -
E. Zwierlein-Diehl, *Die Gemmen und Kameen des Dreikönigenschreines* (Cologne: 1998)

Erimtan -
K. Konuk & M. Arslan, *Ancient Gems and Finger Rings from Asia Minor, the Yüksel Erimtan Collection* (Ankara: 2000)

Exeter -
S. E. Hoey Middleton, *Seals, Finger Rings, Engraved Gems and Amulets in the Royal Albert Memorial Museum, Exeter* (Exeter City Museums: 1998)

Farnell -
L.R. Farnell, *Cults of the Greek States*, 5 vols. (Oxford: 1896-1909)

F.Berlin -
A. Furtwängler, *Königliche Museen zu Berlin. Beschreibung der geschnittenen Steine im Antiquarium* (Berlin: 1896)

Gaul -
H. Guiraud, *Intailles et camées de l'époque romaine en Gaule* (Paris: 1988)

Geneva -
M.-L. Vollenweider, *Musée d'art et d'histoire de Genève. Catalogue raisonné des sceaux, cylindres, intailles et camées* 1-3 (Geneva: 1967; Mainz: 1979, 1983)

Getty -
J. Spier, *Ancient Gems and Finger Rings* (Malibu: 1992)

GGFR -
J. Boardman, *Greek Gems and Finger Rings, Early Bronze Age to Late Classical* (London: 1970; new.ed. 2000)

Gignoux & Gyselen, *BSS* -
Ph. Gignoux & R. Gyselen, *Bulles et sceaux sassanides de diverses collections*, Cahiers de Studia Iranica, no.4 (Paris: 1987)

Gignoux & Gyselen, *DCP* -
Ph. Gignoux & R. Gyselen, *Sceaux sasanides de diverses collections privées*, Cahiers de Studia Iranica, no.1 (Leuven: 1982)

Göbl -
R. Göbl, *Der Sasanidische Siegelkanon* (Brunswick: 1973)

Hague -
M. Maaskant-Kleibrink, *Catalogue of the Engraved Gems in the Royal Coin Cabinet, The Hague* (The Hague: 1978)

Hanover -
M. Schlüter, G. Platz-Horster, P. Zazoff, *Antike Gemmen in deutschen Sammlungen 4: Hannover* (Wiesbaden: 1975)

Henkel -
F. Henkel, *Die römischen Fingerringe der Rheinlande und der benachbarten Gebiete* (Berlin: 1913)

Horster, *Statuen* -
G. Horster, *Statuen auf Gemmen* (Bonn: 1970)

Intaglios and Rings -
J. Boardman, *Intaglios and rings, Greek, Etruscan and Eastern from a private collection* (London: 1975)

Ionides -
J. Boardman, *Engraved Gems, the Ionides Collection* (London: 1968)

Jerusalem -
S. Amorai-Stark, *Engraved Gems and Seals from Two Collections in Jerusalem* (Jerusalem: 1993)

JHS -
Journal of Hellenic Studies

JRA -
Journal of Roman Archaeology

Kassel -
P. Zazoff, *Antike Gemmen in deutschen Sammlungen 3: Kassel* (Wiesbaden: 1970)

Kent & Painter, *Gold and Silver* -
J.P.C. Kent & K.S. Painter eds., *Wealth of the Roman World; Gold and Silver AD 300-700* (London: 1977)

Kibaltchitch -
T.W. Kibaltchitch, *Gemmes de la Russie Méridionale* (Berlin: 1910)

Lewis -
M. Henig, *The Lewis Collection of Engraved Gemstones in Corpus Christi College, Cambridge*, in *BAR Int. ser.*, 1 (Oxford: 1975)

LIMC -
Lexicon Iconographicum Mythologiae Classicae (1981-)

London -
H.B. Walters, *Catalogue of the Engraved Gems and Cameos, Greek, Etruscan and Roman in the British Museum* (London: 1926)

LondonMagicGems -
S. Michel, *Magische Gemmen im Britischen Museum* (London: forthcoming ?2001)

LondonPCG -
O.M. Dalton, *Catalogue of the Engraved Gems of the Post-Classical Periods in the British Museum* (London: 1915)

LondonRings -
F.H. Marshall, *Catalogue of the Finger Rings, Greek, Etruscan and Roman, British Museum* (London: 1907)

LondonSass -
A.D.H. Bivar, *Catalogue of the Western Asiatic Seals in the British Museum*, Stamp seals II, the Sassanian dynasty (London: 1969)

Luni -
G. Sena Chiesa, *Gemme di Luni* (Rome: 1978)

Madrid -
R. Casal Garcia, *Coleccion de Gliptica del Museo Arqueologico Nacional*, 2 vols. (Madrid: [1990]?)

Merz -
M.-L. Vollenweider, *Deliciae Leonis - Antike geschnittene Steine und Ringe aus eine Privatsammlung* (Mainz: 1984)

Mira et Magica -
H. Philipp, *Mira et Magica: Gemmen im Ägyptischen Museum der Staatlichen Museen Preussischer Kulturbesitz, Berlin-Charlottenburg* (Mainz: 1986)

Munich -
i - E. Brandt; ii - E. Brandt, E. Schmidt; iii - E. Brandt, A. Krug, W. Gercke, E. Schmidt, *Antike Gemmen in deutschen Sammlungen* 1: *Munich* (Munich: 1968-1972)

Naples -
U. Pannuti, *Museo Archeologico Nazionale di Napoli: Catalogo della collezione glittica* 1 & 2 (Rome: 1983, 1994)

Nijmegen -
M. Maaskant-Kleibrink, *Description of the Collections in the Rijksmuseum G.M. Kam at Nijmegen, X. The Engraved Gems, Roman and non-Roman* (Nijmegen: 1986)

Nuremberg -
C. Weiss, *Die antiken Gemmen der Sammlung Friedrich Julius Rudolf Bergau im Germanischen Nationalmuseum, Nürnberg* (Nürnberg: 1996)

N.Y. -
G.M.A. Richter, *Catalogue of Engraved Gems: Greek, Etruscan and Roman. Metropolitan Museum of Art New York* (Rome: 1956)

N.Y.Sas -
C.J. Brunner, *Sasanian Stamp Seals in the Metropolitan Museum of Art* (New York: 1980)

Oxford -
J. Boardman & M.-L. Vollenweider, *Catalogue of the Engraved Gems and Finger Rings:* 1 *Greek and Etruscan* (OUP: 1978)

Plantzos, *Hellenistic -*
D. Plantzos, *Hellenistic Engraved Gems* (OUP: 1999)

Pushkin -
S. Finogenova, 'The Collection of Ancient Gems in the State Pushkin Museum of Fine Arts' in *Index Thesauri Gemmarum Antiquarum...* (Moscow: 1993)

QAN -
R.N. Frye, *Sasanian Remains from Qasr-i Abu Nasr: Seals, Sealings and Coins* (Cambridge, Mass.: 1973)

Raspe/Tassie -
R.E. Raspe, *A Descriptive Catalogue of a General Collection of Ancient and Modern Engraved Gems, Cameos as well as Intaglios .... and cast in Coloured Pastes, White Enamel and Sulphur by James Tassie, Modeller* (London: 1791)

RecGén -
W.H. Waddington, E. Babelon & Th. Reinach, *Recueil Général des Monnaies Grecques d'Asie Mineure* (Paris: 1904-12)

Richter 2 -
G.M.A. Richter, *Engraved Gems of the Romans* (London: 1971)

Romania -
M. Gramatopol, *Les Pierres gravées du Cabinet numismatique de l'Académie Roumaine,* Collection Latomus 138 (Brussels: 1974)

RPC -
A. Burnett et al., *Roman Provincial Coinage*, 1 & 2 (London/Paris: 1992 (reprint 1998) & 1999)

Sa'd -
M. Henig & M. Whiting, *Engraved Gems from Gadara in Jordan: the Sa'd Collection of Intaglios and Cameos* (OUCA: 1985)

Snettisham -
C. Johns, *The Snettisham Roman Jeweller's Hoard* (London: 1997)

Sofia -
A. Dimitrova-Milcheva, *Antique Engraved Gems and Cameos in the National Archaeological Museum in Sofia* (Sofia: 1981)

Thorvaldsen -
P. Fossing, *The Thorvaldsen Museum. Catalogue of the Antique Engraved Gems and Cameos* (Copenhagen: 1929)

Tier-und Pflanzen -
F. Imhoof-Blumer, O. Keller, *Tier- und Pflanzenbilder auf Münzen und Gemmen des klassischen Altertums* (Leipzig: 1889)

Vienna -
E. Zwierlein-Diehl, *Die antiken Gemmen des Kunsthistorischen Museums in Wien* 1-3 (Munich: 1973, 1979, 1991)

Wellcome -
R. Nicholls, *The Wellcome Gems* (Cambridge: 1983)

Würzburg -
E. Zwierlein-Diehl, *Glaspasten im Martin-Von-Wagner Museum der Universität Würzburg* 1 - *Abdrücke von antiken und ausgewählten nachantiken Intagli und Kameen* (Munich: 1986)

Xanten 1, 2 -
G. Platz-Horster, *Die antiken Gemmen aus Xanten* 1 & 2 (Cologne/Bonn: 1987, 1994)

ZPE -
Zeitschrift Für Papyrologie und Epigraphik

Index of Materials

(Numbers refer to catalogue numbers, not to pages)

Agate: **31** (layered)

Chalcedony: **6, 39**
Cornelian: **2, 7, 11-12, 17-19, 21-2, 25, 28-30, 33, 35** (sard), **37-8** (yellow), **40-6, 50, 53** (red), **54-5** (sard)

Garnet: **4, 9-10**
Glass: **5, 20, 34, 51-2, 57-9**

Haematite: **32, 56**

Jasper:
  brownish-grey, **27**(?)
  green: **1**
  red: **8, 16**
  yellow: **24, 26**

Nicolo: **15**

Plasma: **13-4, 23, 36, 49**

Sard see cornelian
Serpentinite: **3** (black), **47**(?)
Steatite: **48** (pale green)
Stone: **27** (brownish-grey jasper?), **47** (dark green with mottling)

Index of Provenances

(Numbers refer to catalogue numbers, not to pages)

Turkey:
  Black Sea area: **1, 47**
  Giresun (Cerasus): **9, 31, 38, 54-5**
  Istanbul (Byzantium/Constantinople): **14, 26-7**
  Kayseri (Mazaca/Caesarea): **3, 48**
  Mersin (Zephyrion/Hadrianopolis nr Tarsus) : **5**
  Ordu (Kotyora): **8**
  Rize (Rhizaion nr Trebzon): **34-5, 49, 56**
  Sadak (Satala): **11, 22**
  Silifke (Seleucia): **12, 17, 19**
  Sinop (Sinope): **51**
  Tarsus: **29, 32**
  Trebzon/Trebizond (Trapezus): **4, 21, 28, 33, 40, 46, 50**

Syria:
  Aleppo (Beroea): **18, 57-9**
  Antakya (Antioch/Antiochia): **23**

Yugoslavia (former):
  Belgrade (Serbia): **7**
  Ohrid (Macedonia): **16**
  Split (Dalmatia, Croatia): **24**
  ? Zagreb (Croatia): **2, 6, 15, 36-7**

Unknown Provenance: **10, 13, 20, 25, 39, 52-3**

Collections:

Cook, Prof. A.B. (bt. at Sotheby's sale, 15/1/1952): **41-5**
Southesk collection (no.17): **30**

Index of Subjects

(Numbers refer to catalogue numbers, not to pages)

Ajax: **52**
Alpha & Omega (Omicron): **48**
Altar: **6-7** (before Zeus enthroned)
Amastris: **25**(?)
Ankh sign: **32** (held by Anubis or Seth)
Ant: **22** (with Fortuna-Ceres)
Anubis (or Seth?): **32**
Aphrodite/Venus: **4** (bust)?, **13** (Venus Victrix)
Apollo: **5** (bust)?, **8** (holding *patera*)
Apollo Agyieus: **8**(?)
Ares/Mars: **12**, **49**(?)
Arsinoe III: **4** (bust)?
Artemis/Diana: **8** (with torch(es)), **9** (with bow)
Astakos: **25**(?)
Athena/Minerva: **51**, **53** (head or bust)?

Bacchic figures see Maenad, Satyrs, Silenus
Bead: **5**
Birds: **39** (doves(?) on a fountain), **42** (partridge?), **43** (pheasant?), **44-5** (ducks?)
Boars see Pigs
Busts see Portraits

Ceres see Demeter/Ceres; also Concordia-Ceres, Fortuna-Ceres
Combinations: **29** (*gryllos*), **30** (conjoined Silenus and ram's head), **55** (conjoined Silenus and female head); cf. also Satyrs
Columns: **8** (Apollo Agyieus?)
Concordia(e): **24**
Concordia-Ceres: **23**
Corn: **3** (before priest)?, **29** (in field behind *gryllos*)
Crescent moon: **29** (and star in field)
Cupid see Eros/Cupid

Deities (uncertain): see God, Goddess(es)
Demeter/Ceres: **8**(?) see also Ceres
Diana see Artemis/Diana
Dioscuri: **46**(?)
Dioscuros: **33** (bust)?
Dog: **2**
Doves: **39** (on a fountain)?
Ducks: **44-5**(?)

Eagle: **6** (with Zeus enthroned), **7** (between standards), **21** (with Victory)?, **28** (on altar)
Eros/Cupid: **14-6**, **48**(?)

Falcon: **1**
Figure(s): **3** (priest or worshipper), **24** (Tychai/Concordiae?), **25** (uncertain identity, standing on prow), **46** (Gemini?), **48** (winged (Cupid?)), **50** (holding flag)
Fortuna-Ceres: **22**
Fortuna(e): **24**; see also Tychai
Fountain: **39** (with birds (doves?))

Gemini: **46**(?)
Geryon/Geryones (and Herakles/Hercules): **26**

Wright Gems

Geryones see Geryon
Globes (or moons): **46** (in field)
Goatherd: **36**
God: **5** (bust of Apollo?)
Goddess(es): **4** (bust of queen, Aphrodite, or Arsinoe III?), **8** (Artemis/Diana, Demeter/Ceres, Kore/Persephone/Proserpina, or Hekate?), **53** (bust of Athena?)
Gryllos: **29** (hippolectryon type)

Hawk: **1**
Heads see Portraits
Hekate: **8**(?)
Helios/Sol: **47**(?)
Herakles/Hercules (and Geryon/Geryones): **26**
Hercules see Herakles
Hermes/Mercury: **10-11**
Horus-hawk: **1**

Inscriptions: see **INSCRIPTIONS** below

Jupiter see Zeus/Jupiter

Kore/Persephone: **8**(?)

Lion: **2, 40**

Maenad: **20** (bust)
Mars see Ares/Mars
Masks: **19** (Silenus); (see also combinations)
Medusa mask: **31**
Mercury see Hermes/Mercury
Minerva see Athena/Minerva
Minotaur (and Theseus): **27**
Moon (crescent): **29** (and star (or sun?) in field), **32** (in field)
Moons (globes): **46** (in field)

Nicomedia: **25**(?)
Nike/Victory: **7** (held by Zeus enthroned), **21** (approaching eagle)

Palm branch: **21** (held by Victory), **28** (before eagle on altar), **29** (in front of *gryllos*)
Papyrus plant: **1**
Partridge: **42**(?)
Patera: **6** (held by Zeus), **8** (held by Apollo and Artemis), **23** (held by Ceres-Concordia)
Persephone see Kore/Persephone
Personification (female): **25** (Amastris? Nicomedia? Astakos?)
Pheasant: **43**
Pigs: **37-8**
Pillars: **8** (Apollo Agyieus?)
Plant: **3**
Portraits (male): **5** (youth or Apollo?), **33** (youth or Dioscuros?), **34** (hair tied with fillet), **35** (helmeted warrior), **47** (Helios/Sol?), **54** (helmeted warrior), **56-9** (helmeted warriors)
Portraits (female): **4** (Queen, Aphrodite/Venus or Arsinoe III?), **53** (Athena?)
Priest (or worshipper): **3**
Proserpina see Kore/Persephone

Quadruped: **2** (lion?)
Queen: **4** (bust of)?

Sa sign: **32** (held by Anubis or Seth)

Satyrs: **17-8**; (cf. also Silenus)
Scarabs: **1-2**
Sceptre: **3** (held by priest)
Seth (or Anubis?): **32**
Silenus (heads or masks): **19**, **30** (combined with ram's head), **55** (combined with female head); (cf. also satyrs)
Sol see Helios/Sol
Stag: **41** (recumbent)
Standards: **7** (on either side of eagle)
Star (or sun): **29** (and crescent moon in field), **32** (and crescent moon in field)
Sun (or star): **46** (in field)
Sword: **32** (held by Anubis or Seth)

Theseus (and the Minotaur): **27**
Thunderbolt: **7** (behind Zeus enthroned)
Tibae: **16** (played by Eros)
Tychai: **24**
Tyche: **25** (uncertain identity: Amastris, Nicomedia, Astakos etc.?) see also Concordia-Ceres, Fortuna-Ceres

Venus see Aphrodite/Venus
Venus Victrix: **13**
Victory see Nike/Victory

Warrior: **35** (helmeted bust), **49** (standing), **54** (helmeted head); **56-9** (helmeted busts)
Worshipper (or priest): **3**

Zeus/Jupiter: **6-7** (enthroned)

Index of Inscriptions

(Numbers refer to catalogue numbers, not to pages)

A O (?Ω): **48**
E A V (?): **26**
ΦΙΒΛΟ (φιβλω): **32**

Sheila E. Hoey Middleton is the author of *Engraved Gems from Dalmatia, from the Collections of Sir John Gardner Wilkinson and Sir Arthur Evans in Harrow School at Oxford and elsewhere* (OUCA: 1991); *Seals, Finger Rings, Engraved Gems and Amulets in the Royal Albert Memorial Museum, Exeter* (Exeter City Museums: 1998), *Intaglios, Cameos, Rings and Related Objects from Burma and Java* (BAR International Series 1405: 2005) and articles on engraved gems and other subjects in journals. She was elected a Fellow of the Society of Antiquaries of London in 2000.

www.ingramcontent.com/pod-product-compliance
Lightning Source LLC
Chambersburg PA
CBHW061544010526
44113CB00023B/2793